Women and Equality

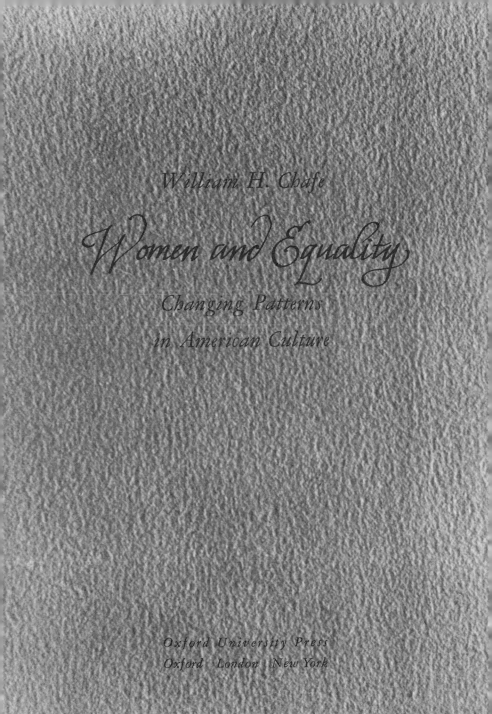

William H. Chafe

Women and Equality

Changing Patterns
in American Culture

Oxford University Press
Oxford London New York

OXFORD UNIVERSITY PRESS
Oxford   London   Glasgow
New York   Toronto   Melbourne   Wellington
Nairobi   Dar es Salaam   Cape Town
Kuala Lumpur   Singapore   Jakarta   Hong Kong   Tokyo
Delhi   Bombay   Calcutta   Madras   Karachi

This reprint, 1979-2

Library of Congress Cataloging in Publication Data

Chafe, William Henry.
    Women and equality.

    Includes bibliographical references and index.
        1. Women—United States—Social conditions.
2. Feminism—United States.   3. Sex role.   4. Equality.
I. Title.
HQ1426.C453   1978   301.41'2'0973   77-15471
ISBN 0-19-502365-X pbk.

For Christopher and Jennifer

and the world they will build

Preface

Together with race and class, sex serves as one of the basic reference points around which American society is organized. Whether we are born male or female shapes our lives fundamentally. It has been made to determine the emotions we are taught to cultivate, the personality traits we develop, our vocational inclinations, the goals we can aspire to, the way we relate to our peers and authority, the responsibilities we expect to assume in the world ("breadwinning" versus "homemaking"), and above all, how we define our individual identity. If it is important to probe how poverty or affluence affects a person's life chances, it is also important to understand how sex-related attributes are intertwined with, and help to pattern, our daily options and activities.

Because sex roles are such a crucial determinant of the way people live, the study of women provides an excellent vantage point from which to gain insight into how society has operated in the past and what direction it will take in the future. Until recently history has been written primarily about those who have "made it." The sources used by historians have been created by people in power (usually white middle- and upper-class males) and the books based upon those sources have largely dealt with the same group. A very different picture results when we examine our common history from the perspective of those ordinarily left out. Clearly we know more about the social system of the ante-bellum South when we look at it from the point of view of the slave community or of the vast majority of non-slaveholding whites as well as from the perspectives handed down in planter records and diaries. In the same way, women's history represents potentially the opposite of the narrow, sectarian concern attributed to it by some critics. Focusing on the experience of the "other half" of the *population provides an invaluable opportunity to escape the limited framework of so much previous history, and achieve a more comprehensive view of the past. Indeed, women's history can provide a unique angle of vision on how society functions and how various groups within it succeed or fail to achieve control over their own lives.*

This book seeks to understand the evolution of the 20th-century American system of sex roles and the process through which change in that system is now taking place. Its principal focus, therefore, is on the nature of social control and social change, with women and their experience as a primary reference. What are the instruments by which different groups within the population are kept in a subservient position? What are the subtle means by which people are discouraged from raising questions which challenge the status quo? On the other side, what are the preconditions for social change? How do people develop a sense of group solidarity and consciousness when they have historically been victims of division and internal jealousy? Through what institutions is support for change developed? Above all, what are the forces which make possible the development of a critical mass of discontented people for whom an alternative agenda becomes both a possibility and a necessity?

The essays in this volume are an effort to explore some of these questions in the hope of discovering new ways of understanding a crucially important subject. Although the essays have been written with a common theme in mind, some may speak more than others to particular audiences. The initial essay, for example, presents a series of conceptual problems central to defining the scope of women's history. Because some of this discussion is theoretical, readers more concerned with narrative development may wish to begin with Chapter 2, a schematic overview of women's history from colonial times to the mid-20th century. The book then proceeds in Chapters 3 and 4 to develop the analogy of sex and race as one way of asking how social control has operated in American society and what the process of social change may entail. These two essays employ comparison, not with the intention of proving a similarity of condition among blacks and women, but with the hope of illuminating some of the patterns of control and change at work in the larger society. The fifth essay uses comparison once again to distinguish the contemporary women's movement from those of the past, and seeks to elaborate some of the connections between social conditions, cultural values, and the development of collective protest. The final essay, entitled "Where Do We Go from Here?", considers some of the obstacles to sex equality inherent in our cultural values, institutions of government and business, and the personal relationships of men and women.

Two caveats may be important to keep in mind in reading what follows. First, although race and class are as important as sex in determining the shape of the American social structure, they do not occupy center stage in these essays. A full grasp of the dynamics of American society would require an analysis of how sex, race, and class have interacted, and particularly how they have been used historically by those in power to reinforce each other and support an ideology in service to the status quo. That analysis is not attempted here, primarily because of the immenseness of the undertaking. Thus although race provides a major counterpoint to sex in some of these essays, and class is recognized as important within the narrative, the primary emphasis has been on how sex roles exemplify the process of social control and social change.

The second caveat has to do with the nature of writing essays. Although historians devote much of their professional lives to working with primary sources and presenting in monograph form their conclusions, there are numerous ideas and reflections which do not lend themselves to conventional scholarly treatment. In some cases the ideas go beyond traditional kinds of evidence; in others they are too speculative or personal. The essay provides a partial answer to this situation, making it possible for the historian to venture thoughts about problems of scholarly importance in a forum more open to the free exchange of perspectives and interpretations.

This book represents my effort to take advantage of the essay form. In the best of worlds, the ideas and explorations advanced here may provoke interest, rebuttal, and additional consideration from those concerned with the same issues. Whatever the reception of the essays themselves, I hope they will be understood in the spirit in which they are offered—as an attempt to record in a flexible framework some judgments and interpretations about a subject of historical and personal importance.

W.H.C.

Chapel Hill
November 1976

Acknowledgments

Throughout the process of developing these essays, my work has been enhanced by the comments of colleagues and friends. If a supportive community is necessary to the emergence of social protest, it is even more important to an author striving to understand the complex ingredients of social control and social change. I have received an extraordinary measure of support from critics who are also friends.

Anne Firor Scott of Duke University has been a source of continuing strength and ideas. Chapter 1 grows out of a dialogue which she initiated in 1975 for presentation to a National Archives Conference on women's history. Over the past five years she has discussed with me virtually all the ideas presented here, and her thoughts—both acknowledged and unacknowledged—inform many of the pages that follow. Peter Wood and Lawrence Goodwyn, two other colleagues, have continually encouraged me to think more expansively and critically about American culture. They have provided constant intellectual challenge as well as nourishment. John Cell, who possesses one of the most rigorous minds in creation, has driven me to ask questions I would not otherwise have asked. His suggestions shaped significantly the final draft of the manuscript.

Various essays have benefited from the criticisms of individual scholars. Nell I. Painter and Alison Bernstein commented on an earlier version of Chapter 3 which was presented at the 1976 Berkshire Conference on Women's History. In addition, Bernstein took time from a busy schedule to offer trenchant criticism of several other essays. Much

ACKNOWLEDG-
MENTS

of the material in Chapters 1 and 3 has benefited from a searching reading by Marsha Darling of Duke. Harvard Sitkoff of the University of New Hampshire helped sharpen many of the ideas presented in Chapter 4. Harry Boyte read the entire manuscript and provided especially helpful comments on Chapters 5 and 6. I am deeply indebted to Sara Evans, now of the University of Minnesota, whose insights appear throughout the last part of the book and whose scholarship has been a continuing source of stimulation. The work of Jacquelyn Dowd Hall on Southern women has also been most helpful. Many of the ideas in Chapter 6 were discussed with Peter G. Filene. Sheldon Meyer of Oxford University Press encouraged the idea for this volume from its inception, and with Leona Capeless of Oxford, has offered many helpful criticisms. Thelma Kithcart typed the manuscript under considerable pressure of time, and in addition, offered important substantive suggestions.

I owe a special debt to Sydney Nathans of Duke University and Regina Morantz of the University of Kansas. As good friends and strong critics, both gave the manuscript meticulous scrutiny, suggesting a number of important changes which significantly improved the final product. Each offered invaluable help at a critical time.

The genesis and development of these essays reflect in fundamental ways the influence of Lorna Waterhouse Chafe. She offered criticism of many of the ideas, and just as important, provided through her involvement in the women's liberation movement the insights and experience that spurred my involvement in this project.

None of these people, of course, will agree with all that follows, and some will dissent vigorously. But without their help, the book would not have been possible.

Sections of the manuscript first appeared elsewhere. A version of Chapter 5 originally appeared in the Fall 1974 issue of *Dissent*. Chapter 3 was published by *Massachusetts Review*, and a portion of Chapter 2 comes from the author's "Looking Backward in Order to Look Forward: Women, Work and Social Values," in Juanita Kreps, ed., *Women and the American Economy* (Englewood Cliffs, New Jersey, 1976). The quotations in Chapter 3 from Richard Wright's *Black Boy* (New York, 1937) appear with the permission of Harper and Row. I am grateful to the National Endowment for the Humanities for a year long fellowship in 1974–75 during which part of this book was written, and to the Rockefeller Foundation for inviting me to a Spring 1976 conference on women in higher education.

W.H.C.

Contents

I.

Women's History: Problems of Definition and Approach

As a majority of humankind, women clearly comprise the largest "group" in the world. Yet they also participate in nearly every other group within society. This simultaneous oneness and diversity has confounded almost everyone who has tried to come to grips with it. Although most anthropologists and sociologists agree that some activities and attributes are characteristic of women universally, there are obvious dangers in generalizing about people who share in every racial, class, ethnic, religious, and regional alignment. To make the problem even more difficult, women constitute the only group which is treated unequally as a whole, but whose members live in greater intimacy with their "oppressors" than with each other.[1]

Nevertheless, the importance of studying women's experience seems sufficiently compelling to justify the effort, notwithstanding the problems posed by class, race, and ethnic differences. As the historian E. P. Thompson has observed about the problem of class, focusing too much attention on what divides people can be a vehicle for evasion as well as for clarification. This seems particularly true when basic structures of power are involved. While it remains essential to delineate qualities that separate women in perspective and experience, it is equally necessary to discern what they share in common lest the emphasis on diversity become an obstacle to identifying larger patterns of control. Since sex is such a primary determinant of the social structure, it would seem shortsighted to lose the analytical potential inherent in the concept of sex roles. Indeed, precisely to the extent that women are connected, directly or indirectly, to the operation of society at every level, and at the same time occupy the aggregate position of outsiders, a study of their experience offers an incomparable window on the internal dynamics of social history.[2]

If this potential is to be realized, however, it is important to tackle explicitly some of the underlying problems of definition that arise when trying to deal with women within society. The first and most basic question, of course, is how we define women as a group. In one of the most frequent responses to that question, scholars have compared women to ethnic minorities. More than thirty years ago Louis Wirth defined a minority as a "group of people who, because of their physical or cultural characteristics, are singled out from the others in the society in which they live for differential and unequal treatment. . . ." Wirth noted that minorities could not be judged by numbers alone, because on occasion they constituted a numerical majority. Rather, they were distinguished by their exclusion from full participation in the society, their debarment from certain economic, political, and social opportunities, the "restricted scope of their occupational and professional advancement," and the general tendency to treat them "as members of a category, irrespective of their individual merits." Although other criteria set forth by Wirth pose problems, there seems little question that on the basis of these characteristics, women qualify as a minority group.[3]

One of the chief virtues of this definition lies in the additional conceptual challenges it raises for women's history. Do women, for example, have their own separate culture as in the case of Jews, Italians, or Poles? Is the shared relationship of women to men and the social system sufficient to give them a common repository of values, ideas, and modes of living, despite their participation in diverse ethnic, racial, and economic groups? Obviously, women have not migrated from a common place of origin, nor brought with them, intact, a set of "foreign" ideas. But is it possible that their socialization as a group marginal to power and conditioned to accept certain roles may have created the basis for a subculture? And if a strong sense of cultural identity has been essential to the "success" of other minority groups such as Jewish Americans, what is the implication of that fact for women and their quest for freedom?

The issue of cultural distinctiveness, in turn, quickly generates corollary questions. Most minority groups boast institutional structures which contribute to the maintenance of a separate sense of community, and provide the interior support that gives a group strength for its contact with the outside world. Jewish Americans built their community life around the synagogue, the Yiddish newspaper, the hometown club, the Yiddish theater, and the garment union. Similarly, the Italo-American community featured neighborhood clubs, ethnic political associations, and distinctive religious festivals. But have women developed comparable institutions? Most historians presume a minimal common denominator of shared experience among females, yet aside from studies of groups like the League of Women Voters or the Women's Trade Union League, there has been little effort to identify those institutions which might provide a basis for solidarity and mutual support. What emotional and cultural role, for example, have church groups, day-care cooperatives, or sewing circles played in creating a sense of female community? Is it possible that sororities, the YWCA, women's clubs, or organizations like the Eastern Star have been training schools for leadership in the female community just as Hebrew schools, theater groups, or hometown societies provided a training ground for leadership in the Jewish community? [4]

A related consideration involves the significance of the ghetto as a central experience of many minority groups. Although most Americans think of the ghetto primarily in negative terms, it has also served as a source of security and comfort to most new immigrants. It does not seem too far-fetched to say that in many instances, the ghetto has been a fortress as well as a prison, a haven in which to seek support and sustenance for the next encounter with the outside world as well as a cage which has blocked progress and personal advancement. Since with few exceptions women do not live together in separate communities, it would seem that this is one issue on which the minority group model falters. On the other hand, the years spent by some women in all-female colleges may have approximated the experience of living physically and psychologically with "one's own kind," perhaps even providing the protective and reinforcing qualities associated with the more positive aspects of the ghetto. Conversely, it seems conceivable that women's experience in suburbia during the daytime hours may generate some of the same isolation and anomie associated with the negative side of the ghetto. Finally, what about language? Do women, as some anthropologists have recently hypothesized, express themselves in a distinctive manner, with a sentence structure, values, and nuances of speech which amount to a language within a language, giving women the kind of in-group tie that distinctive linguistic traditions provide other minority groups? Though clearly not easy to answer, such questions demonstrate how far it may be necessary to probe in order to define women as a group in relation to other groups within society.[5]

These issues, in turn, lead directly to an even more important question: How do women define *themselves* as a group? Although on the surface it seems self-evident that women constitute a definable social category (even if one rejects the minority group analogy), the question becomes more complicated upon examination. Just because people are treated as a group by others does not necessarily mean that they perceive themselves in the same way. Similarly, the fact that individuals act in identical or parallel roles does not demonstrate that they share a sense of collective self. Indeed, even people with an implicit, or explicit, sense of identification with a group may not share a bond of loyalty or solidarity with that group. Witness the numerous efforts at "passing" by individual members of oppressed groups like Jews or blacks. Significantly, the one characteristic of minority groups cited by Louis Wirth which is most problematic when applied to women is that they should "regard themselves as objects of collective discrimination," an attitude that clearly presumes a conscious perception of group-ness and victimization.

In this context, an historical analysis of women's experience may be clarified by distinguishing between two types of group behavior, aggregate and collective. Aggregate behavior describes those hundreds of activities that women engage in which are distinctive in nature and appear to be based on gender, but which do not reflect conscious group planning. Thus women in the aggregate tend to cluster in service occupations, but this is largely a product of external pressures and individual responses rather than group decision. Collective behavior, in contrast, describes those activities which grow out of a conscious sense of group purpose and reflect group self-awareness and intent. Marx dealt with the same phenomenon by making a distinction between class "in" itself and class "for" itself. In the one instance, class was an *objective* category defining the social and economic circumstances of a group. In the other, it was a *subjective* sense of collective identification and conscious loyalty. The latter experience of group identity occurs, E. P. Thompson has noted, whenever people "as a result of common experiences . . . feel and articulate the identity of their interests as between themselves, and as against other[s]." [6]

Within these broad definitions there appear to be at least four distinct stages of group behavior among women. The first applies to that body of behavior where women perform similar or identical activities with little or no sense of doing so because they are "women." A large part of women's history, in fact, may involve the study of behavior which reveals a common pattern, but is not necessarily perceived as a group enterprise by the participants, at least on a conscious level. In colonial America, for example, women cared for the poultry on most farms, but it is not necessarily true that they saw this as "woman's" work.

A modification of this form of group behavior would occur in situations where individuals act from implicit recognition of their common status or identity, but without explicit involvement in group planning or intragroup communication. The notion that there is a woman's "place" rests on the assumption that women will grow up with an almost automatic understanding that certain activities, manners, attitudes, and

7

modes of relationship are appropriate to one sex, but not the other. Thus almost by osmosis, women (and men) develop an interior sense of themselves as part of a larger category of people for whom certain activities are either expected or forbidden. An individual woman may justify her behavior to herself or to others by saying, "that's a woman's job," but the recognition of group identity does not involve conscious or intragroup planning of concerted action. A woman who bakes a casserole for a sick neighbor, for example, is acting at least in part out of a sense that this is part of her "feminine" role, even if women as a group have not planned the action.

A third stage describes those activities that result when women consciously articulate a sense of group identity and act on the basis of that perception, but without necessarily challenging the dominant culture's definition of woman's "place." In this type of group behavior, defined as "collective" by most social scientists, individuals arrive at a similar assessment of a situation and take concerted action. If women organize into charitable organizations because helping to feed and clothe the poor is "woman's" work, they are acting in a collective and self-conscious fashion. An example of such behavior occurred in the 1830's when numerous female reform societies developed to promote temperance and purify public morality. Even though such activities were largely consistent with conventional images of woman's "place," the efforts were group planned and based upon a group definition and sense of self.

Finally, there is that form of collective behavior described as protest activity or a social movement in opposition to the status quo. This too involves a clear sense of group solidarity and collective consciousness, but what is shared is a sense of grievance, anger, or oppression, and an analysis that traces the problem to the common experience of being women in a society dominated by men. The intention of such collective behavior is to overthrow the prevailing definition of womanhood, and to forge a new group identity based upon qualities different from those historically attributed to females or associated with a condition of discrimination. The women's liberation movement of the 1960's and 70's would fall under this label. Within this category of behavior, "sisterhood" is a bond of self-conscious unity rooted in the experience of being exploited and sharing a conscious commitment to change. Within the previous category of collective behavior, by contrast, "sisterhood" would involve a sense of unity based on acceptance of the dominant culture's definition of women as nurturant, morally superior, and peculiarly qualified to be help-mates.

Obviously, historians must be concerned with all of these levels of group activity and consciousness. Although identifying each and finding ways to conduct research into how one stage evolves into another constitute a major difficulty, awareness of the different levels seems crucial, as does attention to the social circumstances that accompany each stage. The mid-19th century, for example, witnessed a decline of the family-centered economy, the rise of women's education, and the development of organized women's activity. How these different historical events were interrelated is a central issue for historians, especially the question of how and when women became explicitly aware of acting on the basis of group allegiance and consciousness. Thus in women's history the issue of explicit versus implicit group consciousness addresses one central question and leads directly to another: how did women perceive themselves at different points of time, and did they accept or reject the dominant culture's conception of their identity.

These questions, in turn, emphasize the importance of understanding the impact of cultural norms, and especially the relation between the idea and reality of woman's "place." How do preconceptions about women's roles affect the way in which people mold their own lives? Did Biblical norms about female subservience, for example, keep Puritan women from speaking their minds? And what are the consequences of acting in opposition to prevailing norms? A correlation probably exists between the extent to which people simply "assume" that women should act in certain ways, and the absence of collective forms of behavior among women. That is, as long as acceptance of conventional forms of behavior is nearly universal, there would exist no need either to attack or defend normative standards. Conversely, collective behavior appears more likely to develop in a situation where social change has raised the issue of cultural norms to a level of consciousness and controversy—for example, America during the 1960's. Such behavior may not be opposed to the status quo (witness the "Total Woman" movement of the 1970's), but its appearance more often than not will indicate prior change which focuses attention on the issue. Also, there would seem more likelihood of a challenge to cultural norms if women's lives contradict society's definition of their "place" to a significant degree, and this contradiction becomes a matter of public concern. Whatever the case, the relation between prescriptive norms and actual behavior seems an important area to investigate, both to determine how cultural ideas affect the options open to women, and to assess how the dynamic between ideas and reality affects group awareness.

Finally, there is the question of how external forces influence the relation of behavior to attitudes. As long as the major ingredients of a situation remain the same, people's perceptions of their activities are not likely to change. Social and economic structures have as one of their primary characteristics the tendency to generate values and modes of behavior that perpetuate, or at least do not threaten, the status quo. Upper-middle-class suburbs, for example, contain schools, clubs, and churches that transmit the norms of social mobility, consumerism, and individual achievement consistent with the development of more upper-middle-class suburbs. On the other end of the social scale, the rules of the welfare system tend to perpetuate slums and to discourage a collective challenge to the status quo. Although change may come from within a functioning social system, it is more likely to occur when the external situation alters. War or revolution, for example, creates new boundaries and priorities, which in turn give rise to new responses and different visions. It is for this reason that what takes place in the "macro" economic and political structures of society is a crucial area to investigate in trying to determine what options exist for groups within the society.

Looking back, then, there are five points that provide a

framework for this inquiry into the history of women and sex roles in America. First is the definition of women as a group in relation to other groups. Second is women's level of collective self-awareness and their perception of themselves. Third is the normative definition of woman's "place" set forth by the dominant culture. Fourth are the actual roles women engage in, particularly as they conform to or deviate from cultural norms. And fifth are the external conditions which either reinforce the existing pattern of social arrangements or encourage the possibility of change. As a hypothesis, one might expect the greatest change to occur when a pronounced contradiction exists between cultural norms and actual behavior, and when external conditions facilitate the development of new social and economic patterns and the emergence of heightened consciousness about group behavior.

Although these observations by no means exhaust the problem of defining the scope of women's history, they may clarify some of the underlying issues at stake in trying to make sense of women's experience in society. Using these categories and questions as a framework, the next essay presents an overview of some of the major themes in women's history through the mid-20th century.

II.

An
Historical
Overview

In the midst of the Great Depression, the anthropologist Margaret Mead commented on the dilemma facing women who wished to pursue a career. A female had two choices, she declared. Either she proclaimed herself "a woman, and therefore less an achieving individual, or an achieving individual and therefore less a woman." If she chose the first option she increased her chances of being "a loved object, the kind of girl whom men will woo and boast of, toast and marry." But if she decided to follow a career, she ran the risk of losing forever "as a woman her chance for the kind of love she wants." [1]

Mead's observation speaks directly to the complexity of women's history. At any given moment, the experience of women grows out of a complicated web of cultural values, specific social and economic circumstances, and the response of individual women to both. Although the conflict between marriage and career was not new in the 1930's, the context of world-wide depression accentuated the traditional male role of breadwinner and the supposed threat to that role of female employment. On the other hand, war produced a situation that made traditional roles seem less important. Thus the worlds of work, family, cultural values, and personal aspiration must be seen in relation to each other and within the context of a specific historical period.

In what may seem a contradiction to this emphasis on complexity, one of the remarkable themes of women's history has been the constancy of prescriptive attitudes toward woman's "place" over three and a half centuries. Especially for white middle- and upper-class women it has been customary to define happiness as fulfilling the "biological destiny" of being good wives and mothers. The historian Julia Cherry Spruill observed that in the South in the 17th and 18th centuries "unmarried persons were regarded as pitiable encumbrances" and that "the home was the only field in which superior women might distinguish themselves." The family, in turn, was generally perceived as a hierarchy, with the man as father and head, and women and children as his inferiors. Although Puritan New Englanders believed that such an arrangement mirrored a divine pattern, with man's role in the home similar to God's role in the universe, one did not have to be a Puritan to subscribe to the idea of patriarchy. "In truth," the 19th-century Southern sociologist George Fitzhugh observed, "woman, like children, has but one right and that is the right to protection. The right to protection involves the obligation to obey." If there was a model of perfection in such a world-view, it was the matron quoted in *The Spectator,* a periodical read widely in the colonies. "I am married," she wrote, "and I have no other concern but to please the man I love; he is the end of every care I have; if I dress, it is for him; if I read a poem, or a play, it is to qualify myself for a conversation agreeable to his taste. . . ." [2]

With some shifts of nuance and emphasis, the same normative values also characterized 19th- and 20th-century attitudes toward women. *The Ladies Calling,* regarded as the most authoritative advice manual dealing with female behavior in the late 17th and the 18th century, instructed women to be modest, meek, obedient, and pious—qualities nearly identical with the piety, purity, submissiveness, and domesticity which the historian Barbara Welter has identified as principal components of the "cult of domesticity" in mid-19th-century America. By the 1920's, Patricia Graham has noted, these virtues had been updated to include "youth," pleasing "appearance," and "acquiesence" as well as domesticity, but the desired end product was substantially the same. When Adlai Stevenson told the graduating women of Smith in 1955 that their task was to "influence man and boy" through the "humble role of housewife," he was essentially repeating *The*

Spectator's 18th-century injunction that women should "distinguish themselves as tender mothers and faithful wives rather than furious partisans." Since women's ideal role was to be supportive of their husbands, care for their children, and provide a haven from the troubles of the outside world, the idea that they might wish an independent life or career of their own seemed unnatural. As one woman's magazine observed in the 1930's: [3]

> The office woman, no matter how successful, is a transplanted posy. . . . Just as a rose comes to its fullest beauty in its own appropriate soil, so does a home woman come to her fairest blooming when her roots are stuck deep in the daily and hourly affairs of her own most dearly beloved.

But if cultural norms have remained relatively stable through time, the same cannot be said for social and economic circumstances. The behavior of women took shape against the backdrop of shifting economic demands, demographic patterns, and personal aspirations and crises. As institutions changed and the contours of the nation's economy altered, women responded differently from generation to generation, sometimes initiating change, at other times reacting to it, in the process frequently dividing along class or racial lines.

In the overwhelmingly agrarian society of colonial America, there was little opportunity for a leisure class existence or a polarization of labor between the sexes. Women from all classes were centrally involved in the mainstream economic activities of the community. Crops had to be planted and harvested, animals tended, clothes made, gardens cared for, and food prepared. Even in households with many servants, the mistress spent her day coordinating work activities, keeping accounts, and planning how best to produce the goods required to satisfy the clothing and food needs of various members of the household. In most cases, of course, it was the women of the family who spun the yarn, wove the cloth, kept the poultry, made the butter and cheese, harvested the vegetables, and prepared the food. The value and variety of women's economic activities were well illustrated in an 18th-century Pennsylvania advertisement. Women settlers were needed, it said, who were capable of "raising small stock, dairying, marketing, combing, carding, spinning, knitting, sewing, pickling, preserving, etc." It was the "etc." which perhaps spoke most eloquently of the demands made on women.[4]

In all these respects, America in the 17th and 18th centuries bore a striking resemblance to pre-industrial European society. In "the world we have lost," as Peter Laslett has described that society, the household served as the center of production and the labor of each of its members was indispensable to survival. No one was without a task, and woman's contribution was essential to economic self-sufficiency. The American countryside was in many ways like the 19th-century province of Brittany described by the French historian Gouesse: "All the inhabitants of the farm formed a working community . . . linked one to the other like the crew of a ship." Visitors to the Carolina frontier saw women caring for hogs and cows, making butter and cheese, sowing and reaping corn, and fashioning medicine from herbs. Women from more affluent families performed much the same work only in a more refined setting. A Northern visitor to the South in 1775 described her sister-in-law's activities: "She has . . . a garden, from which she supplies the town with what vegetables they use, also with melons and other fruits. She even descends to make minced pies, cheesecakes, tarts, and little biskets, which she sends down to town once or twice a day." Eliza Lucas Pinckney, a member of one of the most aristocratic colonial families and hence perhaps most likely to act out the ideal of the leisure woman's "place," in fact contradicted it substantially. A skilled agronomist who helped develop indigo as a mass-production crop, she managed three plantations, oversaw the education of her children, and carried on extensive agricultural experiments.[5]

The harsh facts of demography made even less likely the actualization of the leisure-class ideal described in the normative literature. Many women bore ten or twelve children, frequently living to see half of them die. As Anne Firor Scott has observed, "From the standpoint of ordinary people, the essential theme of the eighteenth century experience was not so much achievement as the fragility . . . of life. Death was an omnipresent reality." Jane Franklin Mecom, sister of the more famous Benjamin, had lost four of her twelve children by the time she reached fifty-one. In the next year a daughter died, leaving in her care four grandchildren, two of whom also died in six months' time. Only two of Thomas Jefferson's six children lived to maturity. So frequent were infant and maternal mortality that many women lived in constant fear of pregnancy. Indeed, in light of the burden of childbirth and childcare and the major contribution made by women to the economic production of the household, it is clear that no more than a few women could aspire to the leisure-class ideal described in *The Spectator*. [6]

Partly because of the prevalence of early death, women also played a significant part in the public economic life of the society. It was not unusual for a widow to find herself in charge of a large farm, merchant business, or a shop. Although the socialization of affluent women emphasized passivity and genteel manners rather than assertiveness and business acumen, the average woman met such challenges with little difficulty. Women ran groceries, practiced medicine, and served as midwives, teachers, nurses, and printers. In 1690 some 40 per cent of all the taverns in Boston were run by women, and, in the same year, city authorities granted more than thirty women the right to saw lumber and manufacture potash. Whether as the result of the untimely death of a husband, or through their own initiative, individual women functioned effectively in the world of commerce.

Still others contributed in notable ways to the world of public affairs. Margaret Brent, a noblewoman who came to Maryland in the mid-17th century, was a famous stateswoman of her day. Already well regarded for her management of huge family landholdings, she was appointed after the death of Governor Leonard Calvert as executrix of his estate. In that position she played a crucial role in resolving numerous political disputes—in the words of Julia Cherry

Spruill, "Rescu [ing] the struggling little colony from certain disaster." Mary Musgrove performed similar diplomatic feats for the colony of Georgia. The daughter of an Indian mother and an English father, she mediated between the Creek Indians and the colonial government of James Oglethorpe, acting to maintain the peace and at critical moments, to rally Indian support to Oglethorpe's side.[7]

Overall, then, a strangely distant relationship appears to have existed between received cultural norms about woman's "place" and the actual content of most women's lives. That the norms were not forgotten can be seen clearly in a note from Thomas Jefferson to his daughter. "Your last two letters," he wrote, "are those which have given me the greatest pleasure of any I have ever received from you. The one announced that you have become a notable housewife; the other, a mother." Furthermore, it was not unheard of for traditional norms to be invoked in a restrictive manner. Anne Hutchinson was expelled from Massachusetts not only for her religious views but for "acting the part" rather of "a husband than a wife" and for behaving in a way "not fitting" for her sex.[8]

Yet for the most part, prescriptive attitudes appeared only indirectly relevant to women's daily lives, existing more as conventions to which homage was paid on ritual occasions than as injunctions women were expected to obey in their everyday activities. Attacks on prevailing norms were rare; but, then again, such attacks might not be pertinent if the norms were not perceived as an immediate impediment to the routines necessary to keep life going. Reality existed on one side, prescriptive norms on the other, and, as long as homage was offered where appropriate, the rest of life could go on as usual. The result was a variety of behavior among women which, although not contradictory to existing norms, nevertheless differed considerably from what one might expect from reading the prescriptive literature.

The dynamics of this relationship were well illustrated in the life of Ann Catherine Green. An 18th-century citizen of Maryland, she married and bore fourteen children, eight of whom died before maturity. When her husband died also, she took over his printing business, assuming responsibility as editor of the *Maryland Gazette* and official printer for the colony. For eight years she carried on the business, performing the same work and receiving the same payment from the government as had her husband. Yet upon her own death, the obituary read: "she was of a mild and benevolent disposition, and for conjugal affection and parental tenderness, an example of her sex." What seems most significant from this brief vignette is that at moments such as death there was almost a mandatory return to traditional verities, acknowledging the fundamental "truths" about masculine and feminine roles and putting things back in their proper place. By such a process traditional norms were recognized regularly, even as in daily life the central role of women in the production of the domestic economy and the struggle to overcome problems of birth and survival made almost impossible the pure enactment of traditional roles.[9] Thus in colonial America, prescriptive norms about women appeared to exist more as part of society's rituals than as a major force dictating people's daily lives.*

Significantly, the major shift in the relation of norms to behavior accompanied the fundamental transformation of the nation's economy which occurred with the industrial revolu-

---

* Although the word "normative" customarily refers to the highest standards of behavior prescribed for a given society, it can also denote the "norm" or "average" of behavior actually found. In the colonial context particularly, it may be helpful to distinguish the "ideal" from the "expected." The distinction helps to explicate the relationship between prescribed norms and actual behavior. The ideal image of woman's "place" that many colonists carried from England remained intact, but the conditions of life generated a set of expectations about women's actual behavior which permitted a much greater variety and freedom of activity. Thus even as the "ideal" was retained and honored, the average range of behavior expected of women differed substantially from the "ideal." In a sense, then, the "norms" or expectations governing women's behavior were far more flexible than prescriptive sermons or writings would suggest. Continued veneration of the "ideal," on the other hand, provided the foundation for a different set of expectations to evolve in the 19th century when social circumstances made it more possible for middle- and upper-class women to conform to the "ideal." In short, the prescriptive values stayed relatively constant, but changing social and economic conditions altered expectations of how women should conform to the values.

tion. From the point of view of male and female roles, the primary impact of industrialism was to separate the homeplace from the workplace. As tasks such as clothesmaking and food processing were gradually transferred to factories, and as craftsmen moved from their shops to larger manufacturing facilities, the household unit as the center of economic activity declined. With it, the central economic role of women also declined. Women continued to perform indispensable work in and outside of the home, but no longer was there the inextricable relationship of male and female labor as part of a common enterprise. As male and female spheres became more polarized in reality, notions of "masculine" and "feminine" responsibilities became more entrenched.

At the same time, the types of activities women engaged in divided more sharply along class and ethnic lines. For upwardly mobile middle-class families, especially, a wife who enacted the culturally prescribed role of full-time homemaker constituted a visible badge of having achieved middle-class status. The price of insisting on such an existence, however, was that wives and daughters of the middle class became removed almost totally from the workaday reality of women from other classes. Rebecca Harding Davis, a 19th-century novelist, vividly described the distance which resulted. In *Life in the Iron Mills* she portrayed the isolation of an upperclass millowner's daughter who each day gazed down from her window at the exhausted faces of workers streaming to and from the mills. Though incomparably advantaged in every way, the rich daughter nevertheless suffered bitterly her own "hunger to know" about the real life of those around her.[10]

Women, of course, were not excluded from the industrialization process which swept the nation after 1830. Young farm girls from New Hampshire and Massachusetts flocked to Lowell in the 1830's and early 1840's to run the looms of the new textile plants. Other women went to work in canning and tobacco factories. Although employment statistics for women in the 19th century are somewhat unreliable, researchers have found that in cities like Baltimore as many as 40 per cent of the women worked. By 1890 at least one million women were employed in the nation's factories, with many more working in agriculture and domestic service.

Yet the overwhelming majority of gainfully employed women were not from those white middle-class families most affected by traditional norms about woman's "place." Although the first factory women at Lowell were native, white, and Protestant, they soon were replaced by immigrants, especially when it became clear that the mills were not providing the healthy, educational environment initially advertised by the owners. Indeed, for women there quickly developed two standards in regard to employment just as there were two standards for morality. It was permissible—even desirable—for black and immigrant women to toil in fields and factories. Throughout the history of slavery, black women had been expected to work as hard as men, hoeing in the fields as well as providing domestic help. The same pattern continued after emancipation, and in 1890, more than one million out of 2.7 million black women and girls were gainfully employed, half in agriculture and half as domestics. Similarly, hundreds of thousands of immigrant women went into factories, did piece work in the home, or served as domestics to help their families survive in the new land. A Bureau of Labor study in 1887 found that among 17,000 women factory workers surveyed, 75 per cent were of immigrant stock, only 4 per cent were married, and 75 per cent were under 25.

By the end of the 19th century, therefore, a clear line had been drawn between the appropriate activities of "proper" white middle-class women and the activities associated with black, poor, and immigrant women. For the first time in the nation's history, women from the former group were not centrally involved in what the dominant culture defined as mainstream economic activities. Their less-well-off sisters, by contrast, provided a major source of cheap and marginal labor. The results were dramatically apparent in the 1900 census, which showed that 41 per cent of all non-white women were employed, while only 17 per cent of white women worked, most of them from immigrant stock.[11]

Nevertheless, the social changes wrought by industrialism inevitably affected white middle-class women as well, spur-

ring new activities and perceptions. Although the industrial
revolution did not directly cause feminism, it provided the
context for the first collective assault on traditional ideas
about woman's "place." Rarely in the nation's history has
there been a period of greater ferment than that which occurred in the 1830's and the 1840's. The movement to the
frontier, the creation of new modes of transportation, the extension of political democracy, and the development of new
economic institutions prompted a society-wide upheaval. In a
period when existing structures no longer seemed adequate
and replacements had yet to be formed, people looked with
new perspectives on the values and direction of their society.
It was a time of religious revivalism, utopian experiments,
and new efforts to move the society closer to the promises of
its founders. People gathered together to encourage temperance, create public education systems, develop new and better facilities to care for the delinquent and insane, and work
for abolition of the most evil of American institutions—slavery.[12]

From the beginning, some middle-class women played a
major part in all these activities. According to traditional
cultural norms, women had as one of their special responsibilities concern for the ethical and spiritual well-being of the
society. Involvement in the church provided one outlet for
these concerns. At the same time, religious sentiment was a
principal motivating drive of the entire reform ethos. Activities in the church thus provided a natural transition for female involvement in various reform movements. As one historian has noted, "the identification of women with
spirituality in revival religion . . . ultimately implied their
special responsibility in the drive toward social salvation.
[This] led to the attempt to realize the ideals of sanctified
womanhood in social action." [13]

But if religion served as a bridge for middle-class female
reform involvement, women activists rapidly developed their
own consciousness and agenda for change. Women abolitionists were outraged when churches denied them the right to
speak in public for the end of slavery. When a group of
Congregational ministers in Massachusetts denounced outspo-

ken women reformers as "unnatural" and declared that "the appropriate duties and influence of women are unobtrusive and private," female activists such as the Grimké sisters of South Carolina recognized that their own rights were involved also in the struggle for emancipation. According to the ministers, God had meant women to be conscious of their weakness so they would turn to men for protection. But, Sarah Grimké had another response: "All I ask of our brethren is that they will take their feet from off our necks, and permit us to stand upright on the ground which God has designed us to occupy." When their fellow male abolitionists urged that the issue of women's rights be discarded until emancipation had been achieved, the Grimkés responded that the problem had to be met where it existed: "If we surrender the right to speak in public this year, we must surrender the right to petition next year, and the right to write the year after . . . what can woman do for slaves when she herself is under the feet of man and shamed into silence?"

Logic and experience propelled Sarah Grimké into a systematic analysis of why women were treated as an oppressed class. The source of the problem, she wrote in 1837, was that females were "taught to regard marriage as the one thing needful, the only avenue of distinction." Consequently, they directed all their energies toward pleasing men by developing those qualities most attractive to potential spouses and downplaying their intelligence, independence, and assertiveness. If women were to avoid the trap of thinking of themselves as no more than "pretty toys" or "mere instruments of pleasure," she wrote, they had to assert consciously their equality and their right to individual development, educationally and politically.[14]

The culmination of such analysis came at Seneca Falls, New York, in 1848 when three hundred women and men gathered to issue a Declaration of Sentiments. A radical plea for the end of discrimination against women in every sphere of existence, the document provided the touchstone for every feminist movement thereafter. Although the number of overt women's rights advocates was small, feminists boldly carried their campaign to state legislatures, Congress, and public assemblies, challenging through their speeches and literature virtually the entire framework of traditional ideas about woman's "place." Because their ideas and tactics were too far in advance of their audience, the movement generated only limited support. But it highlighted the process by which social change on one level could prompt new perceptions on another and create the foundation for a collective protest movement.[15]

The second and numerically more significant response of middle-class women to the social changes of the 19th century emerged after the consolidation of industrial capitalism and the institutionalization of a totally separate "women's sphere." As a new elite of bureaucrats, managers, and professionals developed around the structures of corporate capitalism, the separation of women's activities from those of their husbands increased. Although women continued to spend long hours in important homemaking tasks, they frequently did so without much contact with others. Ironically, with fewer children to care for because of a declining birth rate, and less direct involvement in economic activities outside the home, many middle- and upper-middle-class women approached for the first time the social "ideal" of being primarily wives and mothers in a small nuclear family. As Alice Rossi and Bruno Bettelheim have pointed out, only in the late 19th and early 20th century did childrearing and homemaking become a full-time profession.[16]

At the same time, however, increased affluence accelerated the expansion of higher education for women—a development instrumental in producing a generation of "new women" who challenged traditional sex roles. Throughout the 19th century, emphasis on education for women had been growing, manifested in the proliferation of "female seminaries" which taught both academic subjects and the domestic arts. The rationale for such institutions was the widespread belief that an enlightened citizenry required educated mothers who could transmit with intelligence the values of the society, and perform with skill their tasks as homemakers and moral guardians. By the last third of the century, fulfillment of these traditional purposes had become associated with the newer value of giving daughters of the leisure class greater access to the life of the mind, resulting in the creation of colleges for women such as Vassar, Smith, and Bryn Mawr.[17]

Sending a daughter to college, however, was in many instances like letting the genie out of the bottle. After attending college, an increasing minority of middle-class women expressed dissatisfaction with what they saw as the wastefulness and narrowness of Victorian women's roles. Once having experienced the excitement of intellectual exploration and being treated as equals in the world of knowledge, these women frequently were unwilling to resume the narrowly defined, homemaker roles of their mothers. "I want to go and see something better than I have ever known," Cornelia Phillips, one well-educated woman, wrote in the 1870's. "I want to go, to take wings and fly and leave these sordid occupations. . . . I think sometimes it is cruel to cultivate tastes that are never to be gratified in this world." [18]

Jane Addams, another college woman, experienced the same sense of frustration. After leaving college and seeing the disparity between her education and her daily activities, she began to wonder whether her generation had not "taken their learning too quickly," without intervening stages to make the adjustment more smooth. Her depression increased as she moved into the role of attending card parties and acting as hostess. "I am filled with shame," she wrote one classmate, "that with all my apparent leisure, I do nothing at all." The educated woman, it seemed, had only two choices: she could act as though the college years had never existed, repressing her desire to do something with her training; or she could find some work which would allow the realization of the aspirations she had developed. The problem was that the culture, as it existed, provided little room for such work.[19]

Significantly, many among this first generation of college women created the room, initiating the activities they needed to fulfill their ambitions, pioneering in various business and professional fields, and developing the entirely new career of social work. By the very act of going to college, these women had set themselves apart from their peers. Like members of an elite cadre, they signified by their enlistment a will to be different from the mass. "Only those who had taken part in the experience," a Wellesley historian wrote in 1915, "could know how exciting and romantic it was to be a professor in a woman's college during the last half century." Female college students were infused with a self-conscious sense of mission and a passionate commitment to improve the world. They became doctors, college professors, settlement house workers, businesswomen, lawyers, and architects. Spirited by an intense sense of purpose as well as camaraderie, they set a remarkable record of accomplishment in the face of overwhelming odds. Jane Addams, Grace and Edith Abbott, Alice Hamilton, Julia Lathrop, Florence Kelley—all came out of this pioneering generation and set the agenda of social reform for the first two decades of the 20th century.[20]

Other middle-class white women, with or without college degrees, found an outlet for their energies in voluntary associations. Robert Wiebe has written that between 1895 and 1915 almost every group within the new middle class "experienced its formative growth toward self-consciousness"; women were no exception. If it had done nothing else, the creation of a body of leisure-class homemakers made available a large reservoir of talent to be mobilized for social reform purposes. Some women joined the Women's Christian Temperance Union and campaigned for Prohibition and the end of prostitution. Others worked in crusades for better educational facilities, playgrounds, and juvenile services for young children. The largest number took part in women's clubs. Initially devoted to cultural activities, these clubs became increasingly involved in such issues as child labor, pure food and drug legislation, conservation, and health reform. The General Federation of Women's Clubs, founded in 1889, had grown to more than a million members by the early 20th century, and together with the WCTU and similar associations provided the institutional voice through which middle-class women played an increasingly important role in political and social issues.[21]

The second stage of the women's rights movement built upon the increased associational activity of middle-class women and focused on gaining the right to vote. By the height of the "Progressive Era," career and club women had come to see women's suffrage as a key vehicle for both advancing social welfare and eliminating the inconsistency between men's status and women's status under the law. The suffrage had always been one of the primary demands of women's rights advocates, but between the Seneca Falls convention of 1848 and the Progressive period, the right to vote had become a more respectable and legitimate issue. Instead of representing an assault upon the family and traditional ideas of woman's "place," the vote had increasingly been portrayed as a means of bringing women's "natural" moral and spiritual concerns to bear upon government. In the words of Jane Addams, it was a way for women to become the "housekeepers" of the nation. To those concerned with social welfare issues, the vote promised the means for mobilizing half the population in support of child-labor legislation and laws mandating better factory conditions. To those more interested in politics, the franchise appeared an ideal mechanism for purifying the political process by bringing to bear the sensibilities of women on the decisions of party leaders. And to those who were most concerned with altering the definition of woman's "place," the vote seemed as good a place as any to start breaking down the barriers of sex discrimination.[22]

In fact, enactment of woman suffrage brought few of the changes envisioned by its proponents. What happened was less a change in the definition of woman's "place" than an extension of that definition to incorporate new features. The result was that although women were increasingly active outside the home, the post-suffrage generation of middle-class women continued in overwhelming numbers primarily to be homemakers. The shift in formal legal and political status failed to transform the underlying structure of women's and men's lives, leaving the basic options available to the sexes unchanged.

One of the more important indicators of the 20's and 30's was that the spirit of the first generations of college women did not carry over into the post-suffrage era. Ironically, as more and more middle-class women went to college, the sense of mission and "specialness" associated with a college degree diminished. With this diminution also came a decline in the commitment of college women to careers. As greater numbers of middle-class women attended college, it was the colleges which took on middle-class values emphasizing marriage and the family, rather than the students taking on the tradition of innovation and independence. To be a professional woman nearly always meant putting a career ahead of marriage (only 12.2 per cent of all professional women in 1920 were married), yet during the teens and 1920's an ever increasing majority of women college graduates aimed for marriage. Youth and appearance may have become more important in the twenties than piety and purity but, as Patricia Graham has noted, the structure of social roles remained remarkably constant. Even in politics little change occurred after officeholders realized that women were not going to vote as a bloc.[23]

Indeed, what seems most significant in retrospect is the extent to which, both in employment and in the definition of women's sphere, the situation remained relatively unchanged in the two decades after suffrage. There was an increase in the number of married women workers from approximately 10 per cent of all married women in 1910 to 15 per cent in 1940, as well as growth in the proportion of women engaged in non-manual occupations, from 28.2 per cent in 1910 to 45 per cent in 1940. Still, the proportion of women who held jobs was virtually constant, hovering around 25 per cent. Class divisions in the work force also remained stable. In 1940 as in 1910 the average woman worker was unmarried, young, or poor. As late as 1930 black women and women of immigrant stock constituted a majority of female workers. Nor did the statistics on business and professional women change materially over time. In 1920 approximately 12 per cent of women workers were engaged in a professional life; by 1940 the figure was 12.3 per cent. The number of women doctors actually declined over time, and the proportion of lawyers and architects who were women remained less than 3 per cent.[24]

Despite the suffrage movement, traditional attitudes toward woman's "place" continued to exercise an important impact on women's lives, shaping the experience of both those covered by the norms and those excluded. Women who were not middle class were expected to serve as a marginal, underpaid, and exploited part of the working class; those who were middle class, in contrast, were for the most part denied the opportunity for employment. Coming or going, the twin categories of sex and class exacted a significant toll.

Within the work force itself, traditional attitudes toward woman's "place" infused the treatment of women. To begin with, almost all employed women worked in occupations which were sex-segregated and popularly viewed as "woman's" work. In 1940 more than 75 per cent of all women workers were in jobs that employed less than 1 per cent of all male workers. Nearly three out of four female professionals entered elementary school teaching or nursing. Women in factories were most likely to be found running looms in textile mills, making garments, or canning foodstuffs. By 1930, typing and stenography had become almost completely woman's work, and 30 per cent of the female labor force listed themselves as clerical workers. For employed women, there was clearly a "place" in the job market as well as in the home.[25]

One of the presumptions that went along with that "place" was that women neither needed nor deserved to be paid in the same way as men. The average female worker rarely earned more than 50 to 55 per cent of what men received. During the 1920's and 30's domestic workers took home less than a dollar a day, and women working in Southern mill towns earned only $9.35 a week. Even where men and women held the same job, the pay disparity was wide. In 1939 male social workers received an average salary of $1,718, women $1,442. A male finisher in the paper-box industry in New York City earned $35.50 a week, a female doing the same work only half as much. Throughout, the assumption was that women were working only for "pin money." Since woman's true "place" was in the home where a father or husband provided support, those women who worked were alleged to be doing so only to secure extra cash for frivolous purchases. (The fact that middle-class married women were discouraged from working, of course, illustrated the inconsistency of this notion.) Hence, it was possible to rationalize low wage rates on the basis that women did not really need their earnings to live on. In fact, studies of the Women's Bureau of the Department of Labor throughout the 1920's and 30's showed that 90 per cent of female workers sought employment because of economic need and used their income to support themselves and their families.[26]

A corollary assumption was that under no circumstances should a woman be in a position competitive with or superior to that of a man. Women factory workers rarely were promoted to positions of supervision, and female professionals frequently were excluded from bar associations and professional clubs. Although women comprised over 80 per cent of the nation's teachers by 1940, they served as superintendent of schools in only 45 out of 2,853 cities. Similarly, despite the fact that women made up 75 per cent of the membership of the International Ladies Garment Workers' Union, only one female served on the twenty-four-person board of the union. Consistently, women seeking better treatment met harsh resistance. When women unionists accused the AF of L of prejudice against females in 1921, Samuel Gompers replied that international unions discriminated against any "non-assimilable race."[27]

The other side of discrimination within the work force, of course, involved the almost universal opposition to employment of middle-class married women. In the eyes of most Americans, marriage itself was a woman's primary career, so anyone who tried to combine an outside profession with the occupation of mother and housewife received little support. Being able to "provide" for a wife in the home was a sign that a man and his family had achieved middle-class status. A wife working thus contradicted a middle-class woman's "proper" role and cast a negative reflection on her husband's ability as a provider. Since all women theoretically wished to marry, employers frequently refused even to consider giving women important positions because they would become engaged and leave the job. As one executive wrote in the 1920's "The highest profession a woman can engage in is that of a charming wife and wise mother." With that belief as a premise there was little possibility that a woman of opposite intention would receive much encouragement. Even educators defended the status quo. "One of the chief ends of a college for women is to fit them to become the makers of homes," the president of Union College told a Skidmore audience in 1925. "Whatever else a woman may be, the highest purpose of her life always has been . . . to strengthen and beautify and sanctify the home." In such a situation the woman who wished to be different faced an almost impossible task. Carol Kennicott, the heroine of Sinclair Lewis's *Main Street,* desperately craved a career outside the home, but, as Lewis observed, "to the village doctor's wife, outside employment was taboo." [28]

Instead of changing radically, then, traditional conceptions of woman's "place" in the first part of the 20th century simply expanded to incorporate new elements. On a personal basis, many women enjoyed greater sexual freedom. The cultural changes brought by urbanization and greater sophistication, as well as advances in birth control technology, created a context in which large numbers of middle-class women were more free to engage in premarital and extramarital sex. The flapper, with her cigarettes, free spirit, salty language, and more casual manner, was one symbol of this greater sexual freedom. In addition, the burgeoning consumer economy of the 1920's propelled women into a major economic role as the chief purchaser of service goods—appliances, clothes, radios, domestic furnishings. But for the most part, these changes occurred within a structure of activities and roles that reflected the continuing influence on actual behavior of traditional ideas about middle-class woman's "place." The new attributes functioned within an old framework, so that middle-class white women continued in overwhelming numbers to enact the role of homemaker, even as poor, black, and immigrant women continued to provide underpaid labor for the industrial work force. Guion Johnson, a young scholar, described the world of most of her peers when she

wrote in 1925, that "unless she is a woman of more than ordinary ability and energy, [the average woman] will elect to
do what her neighbors are doing: bridge, tea and gossip. In
an attempt to busy themselves, women have built a complicated system of social rank to which they have become
slaves." [29]

Although it is difficult to arrive at satisfactory general-
izations, there are certain themes which stand out on the
basis of this rapid overview.* First is the fact that only in the
latter part of the 19th century did the possibility of women
devoting much of their lives exclusively to mothering and
homemaking become a realistic possibility. Prior to that
time, women of all classes were too absorbed in mainstream
roles of economic production to have the chance of fulfilling
the normative ideals of prescriptive literature. To be sure,
white women of the aristocracy experienced a standard of living vastly different from that of black women in the slave
quarters. They also had far greater access to education and the
opportunity for personal autonomy. But even upper-class colonial women were inextricably involved in day-to-day economic ventures which were both essential to survival and significantly at variance with cultural ideals.

In the long view, then, the isolation of middle-class
women from men and the workplace, and their exclusion
from what the dominant culture has defined as "making a living," represented an historical reversal. Viewing the leisure-
class Victorian woman's role as an aberration clearly has
ramifications for the way in which we interpret the entire
spectrum of women's history in America. Among other
things, it demythologizes the notion of women eternally oc-
cupying a supportive, dependent, male-oriented, and passive
status, and raises some justifiable skepticism about whether
attitudes describe reality. Although such traditional ideas
have been embedded in the culture from the beginning, thus
providing a necessary foundation for 19th-century develop-

---

* This brief survey concludes in 1940. World War II and the postwar
period are discussed at length in Chapters 4 and 5.

ments, they clearly have not always controlled people's behavior.

Second, the way in which women's actual roles have
changed over time clearly has had an important influence on
the relationship of cultural norms to behavior. Prior to the
19th century the prescriptive norms that allegedly governed
women's activities were quite consistent with the later "cult
of domesticity," but in fact, the exigencies of survival meant
that in daily life the norms were frequently disregarded; they
might be recognized in verbal ritual, but as often as not they
were honored in the breach. Producing a crop, coping with
death, striving to clear a tree line—all these activities made
the traditional view of women as passive or inferior seem
rather superfluous. In some cases, it must be emphasized, the
norms did severely restrict women's independence; but for
the most part they did not directly obstruct what needed to
be done. The relationship that did prevail is depicted in William Byrd's description of a typical backwoods woman: "She
is a very civil woman and shews nothing of ruggedness or im-
modesty in her carriage, yet she will carry a gunn in the
woods and kill deer, turkeys, etc; shoot down wild cattle,
catch and ty hoggs. . . . and perform the most manfull exer-
cises as well as most men in these parts." [30]

By the late 19th century, however, the consequences of in
dustrialism had altered substantially the relationship between
norms and behavior. For middle-class and upper-middle-class
white women, at least, the actual living situation began to
reinforce traditional values, thereby making it increasingly
difficult to circumvent traditional sex roles. The prototypical
ideal of women as nurturant, pious, and removed from
worldly concerns served both to rationalize the new position
of leisure-class women and to prevent them from leaving the
pedestal.

At the same time, the differentials of race and class assumed greater significance as demarcation lines separating the
experience of affluent white women from black and immigrant women. Once the role of full-time homemaker had
become a badge of "succeeding" economically and socially,
the barriers to breaking out of that position became nearly in-

superable. There was the practical problem of gaining access to a non-homemaking role; just as important, there existed the obstacle of violating norms taken to be immutable and sacrosanct by most middle-class people. In the past existing social and economic circumstances had *mitigated* the restrictive impact of traditional norms; now, social and economic circumstances *buttressed* the restrictive impact of the norms, making them vital to controlling the actual behavior of most middle-class women. In effect traditional attitudes now created a framework which narrowly circumscribed the opportunities open to affluent white women.

A third theme is the importance of external events on the relationship of values to behavior, and the response of women to both. Although the industrial revolution affected women of various backgrounds differently, it controlled in a decisive way the experience of women from all social and economic groups. If some women moved into positions of conspicuous consumption and luxury, others ran the looms in the new mills, and still others hoed the cotton plants on the tenant farms which supplied the textile mills. On the other hand, the emergence of industrialism also served as a catalyst for different responses to traditional norms, including the development for the first time of a collective protest against some of these norms. As long as everyone in the society was immersed in the day-to-day process of fashioning the means of production and survival, there was little opportunity to cultivate on a collective basis a detachment from traditional ideas or critical attitudes toward them. But with changes in the industrial process, in politics, and in education also came new ideas, an expanded consciousness and new expectations. The social ferment of the 19th century encouraged the critical skepticism which raised the issue of woman's "place" to a conscious level. Thus the industrial revolution both created a problem and helped generate a response to it.

In this sense the appearance of collective behavior (as opposed to aggregative behavior) seems directly tied to the occurrence of major social change. The initial women's rights movement grew out of the response of social reformers, and especially abolitionists, to the transforming social changes of the early 19th century. The second stage of the woman's movement, in turn, was part of a generalized response from various sources to the consolidation of these changes via the forces of urbanization, industrialization, and immigration. In both instances significant changes in the external environment generated responses by concerned groups to social issues.

Within this context, the experience of higher education for women appears to have been especially important. Acting as a dislocating force, it removed some women from the confines of the Victorian household and gave them a perspective on their own existence and that of their social class which encouraged the drive toward protest. Once the cycle of socialization in which they were caught had been broken by the college experience, it became difficult for such women to accept as a given the "family claim" which was exerted upon them, even if many still operated within a framework of traditional cultural values. In breaking away and pioneering new spheres of activity, these women provided a classic case of collective behavior based upon a common perception and an explicit sense of dissatisfaction. They also provided much of the leadership and agenda for the social reform movement of the early 20th century.

Fourth, although collective behavior itself seems to emerge only in a situation where social dislocation has occurred, the form it takes may be quite different, depending upon the context, the relationship of norms to behavior and the individuals involved. Thus, for example, the early women's rights movement did not involve a large number of people, but their perceptions were acutely radical. Coming out of a movement which itself represented angry disillusionment with the customs of the society, the women's rights campaign of the 1840's and 1850's challenged almost every conventional assumption about woman's "place" and called for a thorough-going revolution that would not only have given women the vote, but also eliminated the double standard in morality, education, and the economy.

In response there developed a different form of collective behavior—that of women and men explicitly devoted to traditional ideas. Rather than ignore the women's rights attack, such people mobilized their own movement on behalf of the traditional virtues of "womanhood." (Of course, neither response would have occurred without the initial social dislocation.) Not only did the anti-feminist response isolate the women's rights movement; it also helped to define the boundaries within which the suffrage movement would operate.

Significantly, the middle-class reform movement which won the suffrage battle did not seek to overthrow traditional values toward women. Although the movement reflected collective dissatisfaction with the status quo, it used the framework of conventional ideas as a basis for seeking change. Arguing that women were needed in politics to bring a moral dimension to government clearly carried different connotations from arguing that the idea of masculine and feminine spheres was itself wrong. Thus although Jane Addams and Florence Kelley and Carrie Chapman Catt were in partial rebellion against their society, they did not assault directly its underpinning of social values. They were de facto radicals whose actions spelled rejection of the sexual and political status quo, but whose words were consistent with, or at least within the framework of, prevailing norms. As opposed to much of the early women's rights movement, then, the suffrage movement represents an example of collective behavior that sought change within the structure of existing ideas with the aim of implementing programs associated with "feminine" values.

In this context, the fifth theme to emerge from this overview is the significance of individual attitudes toward the dominant culture as a determinant of rebellion. As daughters of a South Carolina slaveholder, the Grimké sisters found themselves totally alienated from their culture. They rejected slavery, the society of the South that it had given rise to, and the underlying idea that women had a "place" and that marriage was the goal to which every female should aspire. The act of leaving home, going north to campaign against the white South, speaking out in public places, and agitating both the abolition and women's rights issues, clearly manifested the extent to which their rejection of the status quo was total. Charlotte Perkins Gilman, a late 19th-century feminist who espoused many of the same ideas as the Grimkés, provides another example of thoroughgoing alienation. An artist and poet who had seen little but unhappiness in traditional family structures, she devoted her life to analyzing the causes of women's subjection and devising an answer. Her ideas, though never widely accepted at the time, nevertheless represent the most prophetic intellectual protest of the late 19th and early 20th century. Women could never be free, she argued, as long as they were economically dependent upon men. Only if women could define their own needs and support themselves could they relate to men as equals and not have to conform to male preconceptions in order to secure food and shelter. Power, she recognized, was crucial to the issue of equality, and economic self-sufficiency was a prerequisite to power and control over one's own life. As a consequence, she urged the development not only of economic independence for women, but of new family institutions including day-care centers and central food facilities which would make possible a situation of greater freedom for both men and women.[31]

Not surprisingly, the activists who were more successful in immediate terms deviated less from the culture of their times than either Gilman or the Grimké sisters. Although in many respects Jane Addams was a radical, her allegiance to her family and its values prevented her from breaking away completely. In some senses the choice of the settlement house as a vehicle for self-expression represented a compromise with the culture rather than being a total rejection of woman's "place." The settlement house embodied the qualities of domesticity, nurturance, concern for children and the sick and the poor which were consistent with traditional views of women. Similarly, Florence Kelley, with her advocacy of minimum wages and maximum hours, and her leadership of the National Consumer's League, worked within the established structure, playing upon woman's role as consumer and moral arbiter to encourage purchasing practices which would support those products manufactured in clean factories with high safety standards. In both cases, as well as in the campaign for suffrage itself, the objective was not total overhaul of the economic and social structure, but improvement from within. If on the one hand such strategy facilitated reform and a more positive response from the society at large, it also left untouched and uncriticized the source of the problem within the structure itself.

Yet in the final analysis the parameters of protest are dictated as much by the existing potential for change and prevailing social and economic circumstances as by the individuals who lead the protest. Precisely because the social changes of the 19th century helped to buttress traditional social values, it was difficult to mobilize support for a broad attack on those values. The sociologist Joan Huber has written that "a person who maintains a self-definition with no social support is mad; with minimum support, a pioneer; and with broad support, a lemming." Her insight applies to social movements generally. Only when there is a supportive community to sustain and reinforce the demands for change is it possible to mobilize the courage to counter conventional norms and behavior. At the very least, acting alone requires astonishing courage. Finding a cadre of dedicated sympathizers is thus essential to collective protest and the possibility of reaching a larger audience.[32]

In this context, the college experience of women in the late 19th century was critical. The college years provided a supportive community, a motivating spirit, and a collective commitment which could carry individuals through the discomfort of alienation and provide them a sense of explicit identity. Here, the woman's college in the 19th century appears to have served the same protective and reinforcing function as the ghetto of the Lower East Side provided for East European Jews moving from one world to another. It supplied the security and encouragement of allies, and the sense of battling together for a shared purpose against a common enemy. Yet the possibility of such a community surviving and being successful depended on the ability of the rest of the society to hear and respond. That ability, in turn, was a direct product of the relationship between cultural norms and social and economic circumstances. If the woman's movement did not succeed in transforming the culture, it was as much because it could not have survived had that been its goal as because of a fault in its own vision. In short, there is always a close correlation between a group committed to change and the readiness of a social audience to understand its message. Only if the social context is conducive to an alternative vision of reality can revolutionary protest movements develop.

The final theme to come from this overview, then, is the extent to which collective behavior, cultural norms, and social circumstances are part of a total, almost organic, system. By definition, organisms tend to maintain themselves and to provide means of self-regulation that discourage dislocation and change. As social and economic structures become more established they afford less and less room for fundamental alterations. Thus in most cases it takes a transformation from *without* to create the possibility of major change *within*. The industrial revolution acted upon the social and economic system of early 19th-century America to disrupt the traditional productive role of all women in the household economy and to place middle-class white women in a new social circumstance. That circumstance, in turn, was for the first time in harmony with traditional cultural views of a woman's "place." As that social system developed further, it became difficult to attack it, both because of the absence of a "critical mass" of protestors, and because of the difficulty of finding an audience to hear the message. Not surprisingly, the most radical attack came at the very beginning of the change, not later when the Victorian woman's role as homemaker had been institutionalized. Subsequent reform movements had to work within the structure already established. Thus the suffrage campaign could only modify, not transform, the status of middle-class white women because the structure of roles and values remained intact, and had been consolidated over the preceding eighty years.

In the end, it was likely that a full-scale assault upon traditional values would have to await the development of different social and economic circumstances, a new relation between norms and women's actual roles, and a greater op-

portunity for women to develop a collective consciousness of
both purpose and anger. For most of the 20th century,
however, this possibility was impeded by the multiple mechanisms of social control which worked to keep women in their
"place."

It is in order better to understand those mechanisms, how
they operated, and what they suggest about the process of
both social control and social change, that we now turn to
explore the analogous position of sex and race as issues in
American society.

II

Sex and Race:
The analogy of
Social Control

Prejudice against color, of which we hear so much, is no stronger than that against sex. It is produced by the same cause, and manifested very much in the same way. The Negro's skin and the woman's sex are both prima facie evidence that they were intended to be in subjection to the white Saxon man. Elizabeth Cady Stanton, 1860.

Probably no analogy has been used more frequently by women's rights advocates than that of sex and race. As we have seen, the metaphor first appeared during the abolitionist crusade when white women activists drew a parallel between their own condition and that of the African slaves they were trying to free. Like blacks, wrote the Grimké sisters, women were "accused of mental inferiority" and were refused the opportunity for a decent education. Denied the basic rights of free speech and petition, they were also treated as creatures not able to care for themselves. Ever since, the comparison has served as a rallying point for feminist organizers. It also has appeared in academic analysis, most notably when Gunnar Myrdal devoted a special appendix of *The American Dilemma* to the argument that women were the only group whose history of maltreatment resembled that of blacks.[1]

Yet the comparison has also stirred controversy and anger. Although some scholars and activists continued to draw the parallel during the 1960's, many observers—especially black male activists—dissented vigorously. To equate the experience of manacled slaves with that of comfortable home-makers, they argued, was an insult to black people and a travesty of historical analysis. The issue was complicated even further during the civil rights movement when it became involved in the politics of interracial sex and the emergence of Black Power.* By the end of the 60's as much emotional

* One of the more intriguing parallels in the study of blacks and women is the theme of insatiable sexuality which pervades the folk mythology about both groups. As Winthrop Jordan and others have pointed out,

energy was expended denouncing the analogy as defending it.[2]

Clearly, the comparison of sex to race evokes strong reactions and touches themes that run deep in the culture. But for that very reason it may be worthwhile to take another look at the analogy. Not only is it important to weigh again the arguments traditionally made for and against the comparison. It may also be timely to ask whether sex and race can be seen in alternative ways that might illuminate how American society has functioned to keep both women and black people in their "place." In this sense, the real lesson of the comparison may be not what it tells about the condition of women and blacks, but what it teaches about the process and forms of social control in America.

The arguments for the analogy fall essentially into two categories: (1) women and blacks have shared a collective experience of being assigned a set of attributes and responsibilities on the basis of a physical characteristic; and (2) as a result, each has been denied fundamental rights of citizen-

---

many white Americans carry with them a stereotype of the sensual African lover, endowed with infinite passion and irresistible sexual attractiveness. Karen Horney and Elizabeth Janeway have argued, in a similar vein, that men live in fear of unbridled female sexuality and, faced with their own more limited sexual potential, have found it necessary to control women through the institutions of marriage and monogamy. The two themes come together for white men, at least, in the profound anxiety that black men and white women will engage in sexual intercourse, making the former white male master an excluded victim. The power of the connection of sex and race can be seen throughout Southern history where the fear of sexual contact between the races has been the ultimate weapon used to forge white race solidarity across class lines and thus break up the possibility of bi-racial coalitions. Rape of white women was always given as the justification for lynching black men, even though statistically, the lynch victim almost never was guilty of sexual misconduct. The extremes of hysteria to which the issue has carried some white Southerners was illustrated in a 1958 case in Monroe, North Carolina, where in a game of "playing house" initiated by white children, a seven-year-old black boy kissed, or was kissed by, a white girl. The white child's father went after the black child with a shotgun, police arrested the boy and another black companion, and a judge sentenced them to an indefinite term in the reformatory. Only after a world-wide outcry were the boys released. Such is the power of the sex/race connection as an instrument of social control.

ship, including access to political, economic, and educational opportunity.

The evidence for these propositions seems incontrovertible. Through much of American history, the vast majority of women and blacks have been denied recognition as persons under the law. As slaves, African-Americans were chattel, their work habits, family life, and physical survival largely controlled by the white master. For the most part, they could not own property, sue in court, or move about without permission. Although the constraints on women were less severe, they too were denied legal control over their property and earnings, the right to enter most professions, and the freedom to move their residence without permission if they were married. (As late as 1948 a Georgia court upheld a law requiring a married woman to accompany her husband to a primitive rural cabin—against her wishes.) Under the common law, a woman in most cases ceased to exist legally as an individual once she took a husband, since at that point her identity became submerged in his. Elizabeth Cady Stanton spoke poignantly about the consequences for each group. "The Negro has no name," she remarked in 1860. "He is Cuffy Douglass, or Cuffy Brooks, just whose Cuffy he may chance to be. The Woman has no name. She is . . . Mrs. John Doe, just whose Mrs. she may chance to be." In both cases the absence of independent standing testified vividly to the lack of control over one's destiny.[3]

Even more pernicious than disability under the law was a pattern of informal discrimination which suffused nearly all areas of life. Although black men and all women won the nominal right to vote with the 15th and 19th Amendments, neither group was permitted to enter the inner circle of political influence or to wield independent political power. Both groups were also denied access to many of the social clubs, elite colleges, and professional associations where networks of power were developed and perpetuated. It was in the realm of economic opportunities, though, that discrimination took its greatest toll. In most cases, it was simply assumed that blacks and women belonged in the lowest level occupations, particularly domestic and service work. As Catharine Stimpson has observed, "The tasks of women and blacks are usually grueling, repetitive, slogging and dirty." The description accurately portrays the historical reality of gainful employment for both groups.[4]

Each of these manifestations of subservient status, in turn, has been rooted in the fact that women and blacks were assigned a "place" on the basis of a physical characteristic rather than having the opportunity to achieve a position through individual ability. Stated in another way, neither blacks nor women could aspire to the American dream of individual upward mobility and personal accomplishment because each group occupied an ascribed status which carried with it an automatic set of duties and obligations. Although Irish-Americans and Jewish-Americans also suffered significant discrimination, it was possible for individual males from each group to overcome ethnic prejudice, especially in the second generation. For both women and blacks, on the other hand, there was a visible, physical symbol of difference that immediately triggered a series of responses limiting the opportunities open to the individual. The etiquettes of race and sex have operated on many levels—attitude, body language, verbal nuance—but their impact has been to obliterate individual differences and call forth stereotyped responses. Although most white males have been able to strive for a status on the basis of what they *did*—their occupation, family standing, hobbies, or membership affiliations—most women and blacks have been defined primarily by who they *are*, namely, females or members of the Negro race.

A number of corollaries accompany the phenomenon of being assigned a status, each of which reinforces the analogy of women and blacks. In the first place, both groups have historically been characterized as "ineffectual," "frivolous," "naturally passive," and incapable of performing effectively in the white male world. According to the historian Barbara Welter, 19th-century middle-class white women (and in many cases 20th-century women) were valued in terms of how well they conformed to cultural norms of submissiveness and domesticity. Blacks were measured by the same criteria. Both groups, Carl Degler points out, have been depicted as a different order of human being, people whose intrinsic aspirations and abilities are different from, and less than, those of the "master class." Within the dominant culture, blacks have frequently been referred to as child-like, happy-go-lucky, affectionate, but incompetent; women have been seen as scatter-brained, emotional, nurturant, but without "a head for business." In both cases the qualities which have made up the stereotypes seem designed to leave the impression that the individual groups will never be able to leave their "place." Supposedly, neither blacks nor women have the wherewithal to do well in the challenging, strenuous, demanding world of white men.[5]

Since it has been assumed that these qualities were innate to both women and blacks, a second corollary is that anyone who deviated from them could be dismissed as an aberration, someone who was unrepresentative and unnatural. Historically, women were thought to have been born for the sole purpose of becoming wives and mothers. Hence any woman who chose to remain childless and single, or to pursue a career similar to that of a man could be perceived as "non-feminine" or "pseudo-masculine." "The independent woman," Ferdinand Lundberg and Marynia Farnham announced in their 1947 bestseller *Modern Woman: The Lost Sex,* "is a contradiction in terms." In the same way, blacks supposedly were born to be happy as domestics or field workers and to enjoy serving white people. Thus any protest from the black community could only be viewed as the result of "outside agitation" or of some pathology on the part of the individual protestor. The "uppity-nigger" was as much a contradiction in terms as the "independent woman." Both were seen as acting in violation of nature.

Finally, because of this ascribed status and supposed passivity, women and blacks have been placed in the position of being politically and economically dependent upon white men. In sociological terms, this has meant that they derived much of their influence from association with those above them, rather than from their own independent effort. In the case of women, to be sure, many individuals have accumulated significant power in their own right. Witness the example of people such as Jessie Daniel Ames of the Association of Southern Women for the Prevention of Lynching. More familiar, though, have been those instances where women received status primarily from the men they were related to. Faculty wives, for example, are defined in the life of the university primarily by the men they have wed. In a more clear-cut manner, the status of blacks has depended on their connection with white people; particularly helpful was the white imprimatur that blacks were "good" and could "be trusted." As W.E.B. DuBois learned when he sought a teaching job in the Tennessee countryside during the 1880's, success required satisfying a white superintendent about one's "manners." Indeed, the language used to describe such relationships testifies to the possessiveness and dependency implicit in them. A woman office worker might achieve prestige because of being "Mr. Jones's secretary" or a black author singled out for attention because of being Carl Van Vechten's "protégé." [6]

The strongest parallel between women and blacks, then, has been their ascribed status and shared relationship of dependency and powerlessness vis-à-vis white men. Clearly, not all white men tyrannize women and blacks, and some women and blacks hold greater power and status than many white men. Nevertheless, there exists a system of power and influence from which most white males benefit greatly and in which most women and blacks (as well as some white men) are consigned to roles that are subservient and inferior. Within this system there has long been a perverse dynamic at work which causes women and blacks, almost as a matter of automatic response, to be treated as outsiders and inferiors, thereby giving all those who are not women and black some sense of being superior. Historically, the poorest whites have taken solace from the fact that at least they were not black. Similarly, men, whatever their ability, take pride in not doing "women's" work or having "feminine" characteristics. So pervasive is this cultural reality that it has been embedded in the activities of daily life, from attitudes toward cooking and cleaning, to the expectation that janitors and porters will ordinarily be black. As a result, throughout much of history, stereotyped treatment of blacks and women has been a given of social existence.

If powerful similarities exist for the condition of women and that of blacks, however, there are even stronger arguments against the analogy. The most obvious is that there can be no equating the actual suffering experienced by both. Clearly, blacks have endured more collective oppression, physically and psychologically, than white women. As a group, blacks have been forced historically to live in the worst areas of every community, consigned to the poorest educational facilities, limited to the most ill-paying jobs, subject to poor housing, widespread disease, and, above all, consistent violence. Throughout American history, black people have been the victims of terrorism, including lynchings, beatings, and riots. In contrast, all women are not oppressed in the same way, some are distinctly more oppressed than others, and many women believe they are not oppressed at all. The slaveholder's wife may have suffered some disabilities, Gerda Lerner points out, but she herself participated in the victimization of her female slaves. Thus, "to equate her oppression with that of the slave woman is to ignore the real plight of the slave." Although many women also have been the subject of consistent patterns of violence, particularly in the threat and reality of rape, it is not valid to conclude that women as a group have suffered from physical oppression and overt brutality in the same way as blacks.[7]

This, in turn, is a function of the fact that women live in intimacy with men, while blacks, for the most part, are physically distant from their white oppressors. As Alice Rossi has pointed out, the most striking and ironic fact about women's experience is that they live closer to the group holding power over their lives than they do to each other. Thus, they are distributed throughout the social structure and cannot share collectively the physical experience of economic deprivation, poor housing, and widespread disease that charac-

51

terize the lives of most blacks. Moreover, even if white women do not exercise power in their own right, their intimacy with men gives some of them a closer connection to the sources of power in society than is generally available to blacks. At the very least, they have the opportunity for vicarious gratification. In addition, it is clearly important to most males that the women in their lives not be thoroughly alienated. Many whites, on the other hand, do not care if blacks are disaffected. Thus the very nature of the intimate relationship between women and men ensures that *white* women, at least, will suffer less violence than blacks, will be more acceptable to the society at large, and will be in a better position to influence, if only indirectly, the decisions of those in power.[8]

In all of this, of course, *black* women occupy a position which amounts to double jeopardy. As blacks they suffer all the burdens of prejudice and mistreatment that fall on anyone with dark skin. As women they bear the additional burden of having to cope with white and black men. The black female, the poet Maya Angelou has observed, endures not only the natural stresses of growing into adolescence and adulthood but is also "caught in the tripartite crossfire of masculine prejudice, white illogical hate, and Black lack of power." In this situation, it is perhaps not surprising that black women earn the least of any occupational group. They have been more likely than either black men or white women to hold service jobs. Moreover, because of their blackness, most have been denied the vicarious satisfactions which at least some white women receive through sharing in the prestige and power of their well-off husbands.[9]

But the difference between black and white women runs even deeper. As Angela Davis has noted about slavery, the black woman never shared any of the "alleged benefits of femininity. . . . She was not sheltered or protected; she would not remain oblivious to the desperate struggle for existence unfolding outside the 'home.'" Although much the same thing might have been said of many white women in colonial America, by the late 19th and 20th century middle- and upper-class white women had entered a different type of existence, far removed from that of nearly all black women.* While many white daughters were raised in genteel, refined circumstances, most black daughters were forced to deal with poverty, violence, and a hostile outside world from childhood on. Though white mothers frequently were free to spend many hours in play with their children, black mothers rarely had the time to give their children the "advantages" of Spock-advised attention. When Hannah Peace, a character in Toni Morrison's novel *Sula,* asked if her mother loved her, the mother responded: "What you talkin' 'bout did I love you girl. I stayed alive for you can't you get that through your thick head. . . ." When dying, or running away, or surrender might have been the easier alternative, staying alive was a fundamental manifestation of love. But it grew out of, and created, a situation for black women that differed radically in experience and perspective from that of most white women.[10]

One of the consequences has been a sense of distance and suspicion among black women toward white women. Not only did blue eyes, blonde hair, and white skin represent a hostile force, used by the dominant culture to accuse the black woman of inferiority; but the women who possessed those attributes frequently were part of the problem, acting as though black women were dirt. When Maya Angelou first went to work in the home of a white woman, she felt a bond of sympathy and compassion for her employer because she could not bear children; but the employer refused to call her by her proper name, demeaned her worth as a person, and provoked an angry reprisal. Mary Helen Washington, a student of black literature, has found that nearly all black women writers portray white women as callous, snobbish, and, even if liberal, condescending. Given the relative comfort, leisure, and freedom of the middle-class white woman's

* This is not to overlook or deny the successful effort of many black families to provide a sheltered, protected environment for their children, especially the girls. There is a tradition of sacrifice to provide girls the higher education to become teachers as the only alternative to service work. Still, these women, too, continue to suffer the burden of pervasive race discrimination, as well as sex discrimination.

life, it has been difficult for black women to identify with white women's anger or sense of being victimized.[11]

As a result, black women have perceived racial oppression as much more basic to their lives than sex oppression.* Despite multiple problems within the black community between the sexes, black women have chosen their priorities clearly, tracing many of the conflicts with their men to a racist social structure which denies the black male the chance to realize his own ambitions. Furthermore, the economic realities of the black community have never permitted a rigid division of sexual spheres and roles. Hence, black women for the most part have not experienced the full-time homemaking and suburban domesticity that have given rise to discontent among white women. (Many, in fact, would welcome a chance to share in the life which some middle-class white feminists reject.) Thus black women have approached the entire issue of sex liberation with a different perspective from that of whites. As Mrs. Francis Harper, a black woman and an abolitionist, said over a century ago, if it came to choosing between race and sex, "the lesser question of sex must go. Being black is more precarious and demanding than being a woman; being black means that every white, including every white working-class woman, can discriminate against you." [12]

This difference between black and white women points to another major shortcoming of the sex/race analogy: black people of both sexes come from an historical experience different from that of white women. Before being carried to America, Afro-Americans—men and women—shared an autonomous, culturally distinctive, geographically separate existence. At the root of their identity in America, especially prior to the 20th century, has been a collective, if diffuse, sense of this historic experience of freedom and independence. Thus, black Americans under slavery had a point of reference, a starting place, a memory of something better, which gave added dimension to their experience of suffering here.

---

* Nevertheless, black women have played a critical role in defining the issues of sex and race liberation for white women. The next chapter deals at some length with the role of black women in spurring the development of the women's liberation movement.

Women, in contrast, lack a collective history as a separate group in another place where freedom, autonomy, and distinctive cultural forms existed. Although it could be argued that much of the female experience in America is parallel to that of blacks, the absence of this collective geographical and cultural past is crucial.

In this context, perhaps the most profound argument against the analogy is the differing levels of consciousness about oppression that have characterized women and blacks. One of the primary themes of those who have defended the analogy is that both women and blacks thoroughly internalized the stereotypes manufactured for them by the dominant culture. Thus Judith Bardwick and Elizabeth Douvan have commented on how disturbing it is "to review the extent to which women perceive their responsibilities, goals, their very capacities as inferior to males'." Similarly, it was argued during the late 1950's that black slaves had internalized the Sambo image and had, in effect, become the docile, subservient, ineffectual personalities their masters talked about to visitors and needed to believe in for their own psychic well-being. If women and blacks had in fact identified wholly with the roles they played for their respective audiences, there would be an overpowering case for the analogy.[13]

It has become increasingly clear, however, that black Americans were never unconscious of their oppression, and never ceased, in whatever way possible, to express their rage. The memory of the African past, handed down through oral tradition, provided a strong alternative frame of reference for loyalty and identity. The separate life of the slave quarters made it possible to retain distinctive cultural forms, an independent group of "significant others" for children to look up to, and a relatively autonomous system of values. In addition, whether through plantation sabotage, such as destroying farm tools, or through verbal expressions of resentment at masters in the quarters at night, black Americans even in the antebellum South showed a keen awareness of their condition and resorted to whatever means were available to protest it.[14]

This is not to say that the Sambo role was unreal or had no consequence for those playing it. The fact of having to behave

in a certain way in the presence of whites exerted a crucial influence on the entire spectrum of Afro-American life, including the image of self. Among other things, it meant that the
presence of a white-skinned person automatically acted as a
constraint on self-expression and symbolized the limitations
on the possibilities for self-realization. But the research of
social scientists has shown that there are many different kinds
of roles, and that they vary remarkably in saliency, intensity,
and identification. The role of mother, lover, preacher, or
conjurer is likely to have been more significant and emotionally compelling than the role of cotton-picker. In addition, surveillance is an important force in inducing behavioral
conformity; thus, there was probably a vast difference between complying externally in the presence of an overseer and
identifying internally with such behavior. Field hands on the
plantation might play a role perfectly on demand (warned
through the verse of their work song that "master's in de
field") and just as quickly drop the role when the audience
departed. In contrast, life in a slave quarters or ghetto provided the opportunity to engage in other roles which bol-
stered an alternative, and more internally consistent, sense of
self. Thus, although blacks frequently *appeared* quiescent
under the watchful eyes of whites, and though this behavior
inevitably affected in some ways their sense of self, the evidence suggests strongly a very different, much more rebel-
lious set of attitudes and expressions on home ground.[15]

In this context, the experience of white women seems to
have been different, with much less evidence of a collective
consciousness of oppression or commitment to a change in
status. Conceivably, historians as well as contemporary observers have been deceived by the appearance of conformity to
their "place" by most American women, just as historians in
the past misperceived the state of conformity or resistance
among blacks; but on the basis of what we now know, only a
minority of women resisted overtly their condition or traced
their grievances in life to the belief that women—as a social
group—were oppressed in society.* Through most of history,

* There are crucial caveats, of course. Covert resistance is more difficult
to identify and harder to prove than protest which is identified as such.
Furthermore, there is a long history of individual women who fought

the sense of sisterhood that existed among women seems to have consisted of a shared commitment to nurturant, compassionate roles rather than a collective awareness of injury and oppression. Women believed in giving support, comfort, and sympathy to the aggrieved, but do not appear to have seen themselves as political victims whose shared response should be anger. While public opinion polls indicate that most black Americans have supported the civil rights movement, only a minority of women said that they supported the fight for sex equality prior to the 1970's. For a host of complicated reasons, therefore, it seems that women have experienced less *conscious* resistance to their "place" than blacks have.[16]

The differential in consciousness and protest in turn symbolizes the underlying weakness of the sex/race analogy—the absence of a consistent and collective geographical and physical base for women. In 20th-century terms, the fact that blacks have lived in ghettoes and women have been dispersed throughout the entire culture seems crucial to the dissimilarity of collective protest against discrimination. It was almost impossible for blacks living together not to share a common hostility toward whites or a common awareness of how white Americans controlled their lives and limited their chances for self-fulfillment. Living with men, in contrast, white women especially were denied the kind of incubator environment which automatically raised the consciousness of blacks to their plight. As Betty Friedan pointed out in *The Feminine Mystique*, most women believed that whatever problems they experienced were a product of their individual situation rather than of their social condition. Not sharing a common living experience, they did not have the opportunity to develop a group consciousness of discrimination or a group commitment to resistance. The issue of resistance testifies to the difference between blacks and women, as well as to the importance of the ghetto as a social environment conducive to protest.

---

valiantly against the stereotypes assigned them, and still others who grieved eloquently about their plight without seeing it as a product of collective sex victimization. But it would appear that most women accepted the cultural prescription that they should be subservient to men and primarily involved in the domestic side of life.

For these and other reasons, recent observers have questioned the direct comparison of women as a class and black people as a class. Although examining the analogy helps to bring differences to light, that seems an insufficient justification for pursuing it. Catharine Stimpson, among others, has written that those using the analogy are seeking to exploit the passion and energy of the civil rights movement without coming to grips either with the differences between women and blacks or the fact of white women's racism. It seems clear also that there are important contrasts in the historical experiences of white women and Afro-Americans which makes difficult the establishment of categorical links between the two groups. The absence of a comparable historical memory, differing degrees of material comfort, and widely differing preconditions for collective consciousness and protest—all argue strongly against treating women and blacks as comparable groups.[17]

But in all of this, perhaps the greatest problem has been that those using the analogy have attempted to prove a likeness in the *substantive condition* of women and blacks. What if the question were posed in different terms? Analogies should not be limited to issues of substance alone, nor is their purpose to prove that two categories or objects are exactly identical. According to the dictionary, an analogy is "a relation of likeness . . . consisting in the resemblance not of the things themselves but of two or more attributes, circumstances or effects." Within this context, the purpose of an analogy is to illuminate a process or relationship which might be less discernible if only one or the other side of the comparison were viewed in isolation. What, then, if we look at sex and race as examples of how social control is exercised in America, with the primary emphasis on what the analogy tells us about the modes of control emanating from the dominant culture? Throughout the preceding discussion, the strongest parallels dealt with the use of stereotypes and ascribed attributes to define the respective position of women and blacks in the society. Thus what if the nature of the analogy is not in the *substance* of the material existence which women and blacks have experienced but in the *forms* by which others have kept them in "their place" and prevented them from challenging the status quo?

The virtues of such an approach are many. First, it provides greater flexibility in exploring how the experience of one group can inform the study of another. Second, it has the potential of developing insights into the larger processes by which the status quo is perpetuated from generation to generation. In this sense, it can teach us about the operation of society as a whole and the way in which variables like sex and race have been made central to the division of responsibilities and power within the society. If the forms of social control used with blacks and women resemble each other in "two or more attributes, circumstances, or effects," then it may be possible to learn something both about the two groups and how the status quo has been maintained over time. The best way to pursue this, in turn, is through looking closely at the process of social control as it has operated on one group, and then comparing it with the process and experience of the second group.

In his brilliant autobiographical novel *Black Boy,* Richard Wright describes what it was like to grow up black in the Jim Crow South. Using his family, the church, his classmates, his jobs, and his fantasies as stage-pieces for his story, Wright plays out the themes of hunger, fear, and determination which permeated his young life. Above all, he provides a searing account of how white Southerners successfully controlled the lives and aspirations of blacks. A series of concentric circles of social control operated in devastating fashion to limit young blacks to two life options—conformity to the white system, or exile.*

* Despite the problems created by using a novel for purposes of historical analysis, the interior perspective that is offered outweighs the limitations of "subjectiveness." Wright has been criticized for being overly harsh and elitist in his judgment of his black peers. His depiction of the conditions blacks had to cope with, on the other hand, corresponds well with the historical record. In the cases of both women and blacks, novels provide a vividness of detail and personal experience necessary to understand the larger processes at work in the society, but for the most part unavailable in conventional historical sources.

The outermost circle of control, of course, consisted of physical intimidation. When Richard asked his mother why black men did not fight white men, she responded, "The white men have guns and the black men don't." Physical force, and ultimately the threat of death, served as a constant reminder that whites held complete power over black lives. Richard saw that power manifested repeatedly. When his Uncle Hoskins dared to start his own saloon and act independently of the white power structure, he was lynched. The brother of one of Richard's schoolmates suffered a similar fate, allegedly for fooling with a white prostitute. When Richard worked for a clothing store, he frequently saw the white manager browbeat or physically attack black customers who had not paid their bills on time. When one woman came out of the store in a torn dress and bleeding, the manager said, "That's what we do to niggers when they don't pay their bills." [18]

The result was pervasive fear, anchored in the knowledge that whites could unleash vicious and irrational attacks without warning. Race consciousness could be traced, at least in part, to the tension which existed between anger at whites for attacking blacks without reason, and fear that wanton violence could strike again at any time, unannounced and unrestrained. "The things that influenced my conduct as a Negro," Richard wrote, "did not have to happen to me directly; I needed but to hear of them to feel their full effects in the deepest layers of my consciousness. Indeed the white brutality that I had not seen was a more effective control of my behavior than that which I knew . . . as long as it remained something terrible and yet remote, something whose horror and blood might descend upon me at any moment, I was compelled to give my entire imagination over to it, an act which blocked the springs of thought and feelings in me." [19]

The second circle of control rested in white domination of the economic status of black people. If a young black did not act the part of "happy nigger" convincingly, the employer would fire him. Repeatedly, Richard was threatened with the loss of work because he did not keep his anger and independence from being communicated to his white superiors. "Why don't you laugh and talk like the other niggers?" one employer asked. "Well, sir, there is nothing much to say or smile about," Richard said. "I don't like your looks nigger. Now git!" the boss ordered. Only a limited number of economic roles were open to blacks, and if they were not played according to the rules, the job would be lost. A scarce supply of work, together with the demand that it be carried out in a deferential manner, provided a powerful guarantee that blacks would not get out of line.[20]

Significantly, the highest status jobs in the black community—teachers, ministers, civil servants—all depended ultimately upon acting in ways that pleased the white power structure.* One did not get the position at the post office or in the school system without being "safe"—the kind of person who would not make trouble. The fundamental precondition for success in the black community, therefore, was acting in ways that would not upset the status quo. When Richard tried to improve his own occupational chances and learn the optical trade, the white men who were supposed to teach him asked: "What are you trying to do, get smart, nigger?"[21]

The third circle of control consisted of the psychological power of whites to define and limit the reach of black aspirations. The sense people have of who they are and what they might become is tied intimately to the expectations communicated to them by others. The verbal cues, the discouragement or encouragement of authority figures, the picture of reality transmitted by friends or teachers—all of these help to shape how people think of themselves and their life chances. Stated in another way, human beings can envision careers as

* There is an important distinction, of course, between jobs which were tied to white support and those with an indigenous base in the black community. Black doctors, morticians, and barbers, for example, looked to the black community itself for their financial survival; hence they could be relatively free of white domination. On the other hand, the number of such independent positions was small. Although many people would include ministers in such a category, the visibility of the ministerial role created pressure from blacks concerned with the stability and safety of their churches for ministers to avoid a radical protest position. That started to change during the civil rights movement.

doctors and lawyers or a life of equality with others only to
the extent that someone holds forth these ideals as viable possibilities.

Within this realm of social psychology, white Southerners
exerted a pervasive and insidious control upon blacks. When
Richard took his first job in a white household, he was given
a bowl of molasses with mold on it for breakfast, even as his
employers ate bacon and eggs. The woman he worked for
asked what grade he was in, and when he replied the seventh,
she asked, "Then why are you going to school?" When he
further answered, "Well, I want to be a writer," she responded: "You'll never be a writer . . . who on earth put such
ideas into your nigger head?" By her response, the woman attempted to undercut whatever sense of possibility Richard or
other young blacks might have entertained for such a career.
In effect, the woman had defined from a white perspective
the outer boundaries of a black person's reality. As Richard
noted, "She had assumed that she knew my place in life,
what I felt, what I ought to be, and I resented it with all my
heart. . . . perhaps I would never be a writer; but I did not
want her to say so." In his own time Richard Wright was
able to defy the limits set upon his life by white people. But
for the overwhelming majority of his fellow blacks, the ability of whites to intimidate them psychologically diminished
the chance that they would be able to aspire realistically to a
life other than that assigned them within a white racist social
structure.[22]

The most devastating control of all, however, was that exercised by the black community itself out of self-defense. In
the face of a world managed at every level by white power, it
became an urgent necessity that black people train each other
to adapt in order to survive. Thus the most profound and effective socialization toward accepting the racial status quo
came from Richard's own family and peer group. It was
Richard's mother who slapped him into silence "out of her
own fear" when he asked why they had not fought back after
Uncle Hoskins's lynching. To even ask the question posed a
threat to safety. Similarly, it was Richard's Uncle Tom who

insisted that Richard learn, almost by instict, how to be ac-
commodating. If Richard did not learn, the uncle said, he
would never amount to anything and would end up on the
gallows. Indeed, Richard would survive only if somebody
broke his spirit and set the "proper" example.[23]

The instances of social control from within the black community abound in Wright's *Black Boy*. It was not only the
white employer, but almost every black he knew, who opposed Richard's writing aspirations. "From no quarter," he
recalled, "with the exception of the Negro newspaper editor,
had there come a single encouraging word . . . I felt that I
had committed a crime. Had I been aware of the full extent
to which I was pushing against the current of my environment, I would have been frightened altogether out of my at-
tempts at writing." The principal of his school urged vehemently that Richard give a graduation speech written by the
principal rather than by Richard himself so that the proper
tone of accommodation could be struck; the reward for going
along was a possible teaching job. Griggs, Richard's best
friend, was perhaps the most articulate in demanding that
Richard control his instincts. "You're black and you don't act
a damn bit like it." When Richard replied, "Oh Christ, I
can't be a slave," Griggs responded with the ultimate lesson
of reality: "But you've got to eat . . . when you are in front
of white people, think before you act, think before you speak
. . . you may think I'm an Uncle Tom, but I'm not. I hate
these white people, hate them with all my heart. But I can't
show it; if I did, they'd kill me." No matter where he went
or whom he talked to in his own community, Richard found,
not support for his protest, but the warning that he must
behave externally in the manner white people expected.
Whatever the hope of ultimate freedom, survival was the immediate necessity. One could not fight another day if one was
not alive.[24]

Paradoxically, even the outlets for resistance within the
system provided a means of reinforcing it. There were many
ways of expressing unhappiness with one's lot, and all were
essential to let off steam. The gang on the corner constantly

verbalized resentment and anger against the white oppressor. Yet the very fact that the anger had to be limited to words and out of the earshot of whites meant that in practical terms it was ineffectual. Humor was another form of resistance. Richard and his friends joked that, if they ate enough black-eyed peas and buttermilk, they would defeat their white enemies in a race riot with "poison gas." But the end of the joke was an acknowledgment that the only way in reality to cope with the "mean" white folks was to leave.[25]

Indeed, the most practical form of resistance—petty theft—almost seemed a ploy by white people to perpetuate the system. Just as modern-day department store owners tolerate a certain degree of employee theft as a means of making the workers think they are getting away with something so they will not demand higher wages, so white employers of black people appear to have intentionally closed their eyes to a great deal of minor stealing. By giving blacks a small sense of triumph, white employers were able to tie them even more closely into the system, and prevent them from contemplating outright defiance. As Wright observed: [26]

> No Negroes in my environment had ever thought of organizing . . . and petitioning their white employers for higher wages . . . They knew that the whites would have retaliated with swift brutality. So, pretending to conform to the laws of the whites, grinning, bowing, they let their fingers stick to what they could touch. And the whites seemed to like it.
>
> But I, who stole nothing, who wanted to look them straight in the face, who wanted to talk and act like a man, inspired fear in them. The southern whites would rather have had Negroes who stole work for them than Negroes who knew, however dimly, the worth of their own humanity. Hence, whites placed a premium upon black deceit; they encouraged irresponsibility, and their rewards were bestowed upon us blacks in the degree that we could make them feel safe and superior.

From a white point of view, a minor exercise of indirect and devious power by blacks was a small price to pay for maintaining control over the entire system. Thus, whites held the power to define black people's options, even to the point of controlling their modes of resistance.*

The result of all this was a system that functioned smoothly, with barely a trace of overt protest or dissension. Everyone seemed outwardly content with their place. At a very early age, Wright observed, "the white boys and the black boys began to play our traditional racial roles as though we had been born to them, as though it was in our blood, as though we were guided by instinct." For most people, the impact of a pervasive system of social control was total: resignation, a lowering of aspirations, a recognition of the bleakness of the future and the hopelessness of trying to achieve major change. In Wright's images life was like a train on a track; once headed in a given direction, there was little possibility of changing one's course.[27]

Wright himself, of course, was the exception. "Somewhere in the dead of the southern night," he observed, "my life had switched onto the wrong track, and without my knowing it, the locomotive of my heart was rushing down a dangerously steep slope, heading for a collision, heedless of the warning red lights that blinked all about me, the sirens and the bells and the screams that filled the air." Wright had chosen the road of exile, of acute self-consciousness and alienation. For most blacks of his era, though, the warning red lights, the sirens, the bells, and the screams produced at least outward conformity to the status quo. In the face of forms of social control which effectively circumscribed one's entire life, there seemed no other choice.[28]

---

* It is important to remember that there existed a life in the black community less susceptible to white interference on a daily basis. Black churches, lodges, and family networks provided room for individual self-expression and supplied emotional reinforcement and sustenance. In this connection it is no accident that black institutions are strongest in the South where, until recently, the vast majority of blacks resided. On the other hand, the freedom which did exist came to a quick end wherever blacks attempted to enter activities, occupations, or areas of aspiration involving whites, or defined as white-controlled. Thus even the realm where freedom existed was partially a reflection of white control.

Obviously, women have not experienced overtly and directly the same kind of consistent physical intimidation that served so effectively to deter the black people of Richard Wright's childhood from resisting their condition. On the other hand, it seems clear that the physical strength and alleged dominance of men have been an important instrument of controlling women's freedom of action. The traditional image of the male as "protector" owes a great deal to the notion that women cannot defend themselves and that men must therefore take charge of their lives physically. The same notion of male strength has historically been responsible for restricting jobs involving heavy labor to men. Nor is the fear with which women view the potential of being struck or raped by a male lover, husband, or attacker an insignificant reality in determining the extent to which women historically have accepted the dominance of the men in their lives. Richard Wright observed that "the things that influenced my conduct . . . did not have to happen to me directly; I needed but to hear of them to feel their full effect . . ." Similarly, women who have grown up with the image of powerful and potentially violent men need not have experienced a direct attack to share a sense of fear and intimidation. "Strength," the psychologist Jerome Kagan has observed, "is a metaphor for power." Thus, despite the substantive difference in the way women and blacks have been treated, the form of social control represented by physical strength has operated similarly for both groups.[29]

An even stronger case can be made for the way in which economic controls have succeeded in keeping blacks and women in their place. In 1898 Charlotte Perkins Gilman argued in *Women and Economics* that the root of women's subjection was their economic dependency on men. As long as women were denied the opportunity to earn their own living, she argued, there could never be equality between the sexes. The fact that women had to please their mates, both sexually and through other services, to ensure their survival made honest communication and mutual respect impossible. The prospect of a "present" from a generous husband, or a new car or clothes, frequently served to smooth over conflict, while the implicit threat of withholding such favors could be used to discourage carrying conflict too far.[30]

In fact, the issue of women not controlling their own money has long been one of the most painful and humiliating indexes of inequality between the sexes, especially in the middle class. Since money symbolizes power, having to ask others for it signifies subservience and an inferior status. Carol Kennicott, the heroine of Sinclair Lewis's *Main Street,* recognized the problem. After begging prettily for her household expenses early in her marriage, she started to demand her own separate funds. "What was a magnificent spectacle of generosity to you," she told her husband, "was a humiliation to me. You *gave* me money—gave it to your mistress if she was complaisant." Beth Phail, a character in Marge Piercy's novel *Small Changes,* experienced the same conflict with her husband, who was immediately threatened by the idea of her economic autonomy. Indeed, few examples of psychological control seem more pointed than those represented in husbands' treating their wives as not mature enough to handle their own money.[31]

Even the women who held jobs reflected the pattern by which economic power was used to control women's freedom of action. Almost all women workers were concentrated in a few occupations delineated as "woman's" work. As secretaries, waitresses, cooks, and domestic workers, women on the job conformed to the "service" image of their sex. Significantly, the highest status jobs available—nurses and teachers—tended to reinforce a traditional image of women and the status quo between the sexes, just as the highest jobs available within the black community—teachers and civil servants—reinforced a pattern of accommodation with the existing white power structure. Any woman who chose a "man's job" automatically risked a loss of approval, if not total hostility. For most, the option simply did not exist.

Even those in the most prestigious positions illustrated how money could be used as an instrument of social control. If they were to succeed in raising funds, college administrators in black and women's schools frequently found that they had to shape their programs in conformity to social values that buttressed the status quo. Booker T. Washington represented the most outstanding example of this phenomenon. Repeatedly he was forced to appease white racist presumptions in order to get another donation for Tuskegee. As the funnel through which all white philanthropic aid to blacks was channeled, Washington had to ensure that no money would be spent in a way which might challenge the political values of his contributors, even though privately he fought those political values. But Washington was not alone. During the 1830's Mary Lyons, head of Mt. Holyoke Seminary, agreed not to attend trustee meetings lest she offend male sensibilities, and Mary Alice Baldwin, the very effective leader of the Women's College of Duke University, felt it necessary to pay homage to the conservative tradition of "the Southern lady" as the price for sustaining support of women's education at Duke.[32]

In all of these instances, economic controls functioned in parallel ways to limit the freedom of women and blacks. If a group is assigned a "place," there are few more effective ways of keeping it there than economic dependency. Not only must the group in question conform to the expectations of the dominant class in order to get money to live; those who would do otherwise are discouraged by the fact that no economic incentives exist to reward those who challenge the status quo. The absence of financial support for those who dare to deviate from prescribed norms has served well to perpetuate the status quo in the condition of both women and blacks. "I don't want to be a slave," Richard Wright observed. "But you have to eat," Griggs replied.

The strongest parallel, however, consists of the way in which blacks and women have been given the psychological message that they should be happy with their "place." In both instances, this form of control has effectively limited aspiration to non-conventional roles. Although Beth Phail of *Small Changes* wanted to go to college and law school, her family insisted that her highest aspiration should be marriage and homemaking. A woman should not expect a career. Similarly, when Carol Kennicott told her college boy friend, "I want to do something with my life," he responded eagerly:

"What's better than making a comfy home and bringing up some cute kids . . . ?" The small town atmosphere of Gopher Prairie simply reinforced the pressure to conform. Carol was expected to be a charming hostess, a dutiful wife, and a good homemaker, but not a career woman. Thus, as Sinclair Lewis observed, she was a "woman with a working brain and no work." The messages Carol received from her surroundings were not designed to give her high self-esteem. Her husband called her "an extravagant little rabbit," and his poker partners, she noted, simply expected her "to wait on them like a servant." [33]

Although Carol's personality was atypical, her social experience was not. When high school girls entertained the possibility of a career, they were encouraged to be nurses, not doctors. The qualities that received the most praise were those traditionally associated with being a "lady," not an assertive individual ready to face the world. Significantly, both women and blacks were the victims of two devices designed to discourage non-conformity. Those who sought to protest their status, for example, were subjected to ridicule and caricature. The black protestor was almost certain to be identified with subversive activity, just as the women's rights advocate was viewed as unsexed and a saboteur of the family. (Ordinary blacks and females were subject to a gentler form of humor, no less insidious, as in the characters of Amos 'n Andy's "King Fish" or Lucille Ball's "Lucy.") In addition, it was not uncommon for blacks to be set against blacks and women against women in a competition which served primarily the interests of the dominant group. According to Judith Bardwick and Elizabeth Douvan, girls are socialized to use oblique forms of aggression largely directed at other females, while men's aggression is overt. The stereotype of women doing devious battle over an attractive man is an ingrained part of our folk tradition. Nor is the "divide and conquer" strategy a stranger to the history of black people, as when white workers sowed seeds of suspicion between Richard Wright and another black worker in order to make them fight each other for the entertainment of whites. [34]

In both cases the psychological form of social control has

operated in a similar fashion. The aspirations, horizons, and self-images of blacks and women have been defined by others in a limiting and constrictive way. More often that not, the result historically has been an acceptance of society's perception of one's role. The prospect of becoming an architect, an engineer, or a carpenter is not easy to sustain in an environment where the very idea is dismissed as foolish or unnatural. Instead of encouragement to aspire to new horizons of achievement, the message transmitted to blacks and women has been the importance of finding satisfaction with the status quo.

But in the case of women, as with blacks, the most effective instrument of continued control has been internal pressure from the group itself. From generation to generation, mothers teach daughters to please men, providing the instruction that prepares the new generation to assume the roles of mothers and housewives. Just as blacks teach each other how to cope with "whitey" and survive within the system, women school each other in how to win a man, how to appear charming, where to "play a role" in order to avoid alienating a potential husband. When Beth in *Small Changes* rebelled against her husband and fought the idea of tying herself down with a child, it was the other women in her family who urged her to submit and at least give the *appearance* of accepting the role expected of her.[35]

In fact, dissembling in order to conform to social preconceptions has been a frequent theme of women's socialization. As Mirra Komarovsky has demonstrated, college women in the 1940's were taught to hide their real ability in order to make their male friends feel superior. "My mother thinks that it is very nice to be smart in college," one of Komarovsky's students noted, "but only if it doesn't take too much effort. She always tells me not to be too intellectual on dates, to be clever in a light sort of way." It is not difficult to imagine one woman saying to another as Griggs said to Richard Wright, "When you are around white people [men] you have to act the part that they expect you to act." Even if deception was the goal, however, the underlying fact was that members of the "oppressed" group acted as accomplices in perpetuating the status quo.[36]

The most effective device for maintaining internal group discipline was to ostracize those who did not conform. Richard Wright found himself singled out for negative treatment because he refused to accept authority and to smile and shuffle before either his teachers or white people. Beth Phail was roundly condemned by her sisters and mother for not pleasing her husband, and above all for not agreeing to have a child. And Carol Kennicott received hostile glances when she violated her "place" by talking politics with men or seeking to assume a position of independent leadership in the community of Gopher Prairie. The disapproval of her female peers was the most effective weapon used to keep her in line, and, when it appeared that she finally was going to have a child, her women friends applauded the fact that in becoming a mother she would finally get over all her strange ideas and settle down. As Sinclair Lewis observed, "She felt that willy-nilly she was being initiated into the assembly of housekeepers; with the baby for hostage, she would never escape." [37]

The pressure of one's own group represented a double burden. In an environment where success was defined as marriage, and fulfillment as being a happy homemaker, it was hard enough to fight the tide in the first place. If one did, however, there was the additional problem of being seen as a threat to all the other members of the group who had conformed. The resistance of blacks toward Richard Wright and of women toward Carol Kennicott becomes more understandable in light of the fact that in both cases the individual protestors, through their refusal to play the game according to the rules, were also passing judgment on those who accepted the status quo. Thus, historically, women and blacks have kept each other in line not only as a means of group self-defense—protecting the new generation from harm and humiliation—but also as a means of maintaining self-respect by defending the course they themselves have chosen.

Indeed, for women as well as for blacks, even the vehicles for expressing resentment became reinforcements of the status quo. For both groups, the church provided a central emotional outlet—a place where solidarity with one's own kind could be found, and where some protest was possible. Women's church groups provided not only a means of seeking reform in the larger society but also for talking in confidence to other women about the frustrations of being a woman in a male-dominated society. What social humorists have called "hen-sessions" were in fact group therapy encounters where women had a chance to voice their gripes. Humor was frequently a vehicle for expressing a bitter-sweet response to one's situation, bemoaning, even as one laughed, the pain of being powerless. But as in the case with blacks, venting one's emotions about a life situation—although necessary for survival—was most often an instrument for coping with the situation, rather than for changing it.

Perhaps the most subversive and destructive consequence of a pervasive system of social control is how it permeates every action, so that even those who are seeking to take advantage of the "enemy" end up supporting the system. When Shorty, the elevator man in *Black Boy* known for his wit and hostility to whites, needed some money for lunch one day, he told a white man he would not move the elevator until he got a quarter. "I'm hungry, Mr. White Man. I'm dying for a quarter," Shorty said. The white man responded by asking what Shorty would do for a quarter. "You can kick me for a quarter," Shorty said, bending over. At the end of the elevator ride, Shorty had his quarter. "This monkey's got the peanuts," he said. Shorty was right. He had successfully used racial stereotypes and his own role as a buffoon to get himself some lunch money. But in the process, the entire system of racial imbalance had been strengthened.[38]

Similar patterns run through the history of women's relationships to men. The coquette role is only the most extreme example of a type of manipulative behavior by women that seems to confirm invidious stereotypes. In the classic case of a wife trying to persuade her husband to go along with a desired course of action, the woman may play up to a man's vanity and reinforce his stereotyped notions about being a tower of strength and in control. Similarly, a female employee wishing advancement may adopt a flirtatious attitude toward a male superior. By playing a semi-seductive role and implying a form of sexual payoff for services rendered, she may achieve her immediate goal. But in each of these cases, the price is to become more entrapped in a set of distorted and unequal sex role stereotypes. The fact that overt power is not available and that the ability to express oneself honestly and openly has been denied leads to the use of covert and manipulative power. Thus, a woman may play dumb or a black may act deferential—conforming in each case to a stereotype—as a means of getting his or her way. But the result is pathological power that simply perpetuates the disease. The irony is that, even in trying to outwit the system of social control, the system prevails.

Basic to the entire system, of course, has been the extent to which a clearly defined role was "woven into the texture of things." For blacks the crucial moment might come as soon as they developed an awareness of whites. In the case of women, it more likely took place at puberty when the need to begin pleasing potential husbands was emphasized. In either case, what Richard Wright said about the process of socialization could be said of both groups. "I marveled," he wrote: [39]

> at how smoothly the black boys [women] acted out the role . . . mapped out for them. Most of them were not conscious of living a special, separate, stunted way of life. Yet I knew that in some period of their growing up—a period that they had no doubt forgotten—there had been developed in them a delicate, sensitive controlling mechanism that shut off their minds and emotions from all that the white race [society] had said was taboo. Although they lived in America where in theory there existed equality of opportunity, they knew unerringly what to aspire to and what not to aspire to.

The corollary for both women and blacks, at least metaphorically, has been that those unable or unwilling to accept the role prescribed for them have been forced into a form of physical or spiritual exile. Richard Wright understood that continued accommodation with the white Southern system of racial oppression would mean the destruction of his integrity and individuality. "Ought one to surrender to authority even

if one believed that that authority was wrong?" Wright
asked. "If the answer was yes, then I knew that I would
always be wrong, because I could never do it. . . . How
could one live in a world in which one's mind and perceptions meant nothing and authority and tradition meant every-
thing?" The only alternative to psychological death was exile,
and Wright pursued that course, initially in Chicago, later in
Paris. In her own way Carol Kennicott attempted the same
journey. "I've got to find out what my work is," she told her
husband. "I've been ruled too long by fear of being called
things. I'm going away to be quiet and think. I'm—I'm
going. I have a right to my own life." And Beth Phail finally
fled her home and family because it was the only way to grow
up, to find out what "she wanted," to learn how to be a person in her own right in the world.[40]

Although in reality only a few blacks and women took the
exact course adopted by Richard Wright, Carol Kennicott,
and Beth Phail, all those who chose to resist the status quo
shared to some extent in the metaphor of exile. Whether the
person was a feminist like Charlotte Perkins Gilman, a pioneer career woman such as Elizabeth Blackwell, a runaway slave
like Frederick Douglass, or a bold race leader like W. E. B.
DuBois, the act of challenging prevailing norms meant living on the edge of alienation and apart from the security of
those who accepted the status quo. Until and unless protest
generated its own community of support which could provide
a substitute form of security and reinforcement, the act of
deviance promised to be painful and solitary.

This condition, in turn, reflected an experience of margin-
ality which many blacks and women shared. In sociological
terms, the "marginal" personality is someone who moves in
and out of different groups and is faced with the difficulty of
adjusting behavior to the norms of the different groups. By
definition, most blacks and most women have participated in
that experience, especially as they have been required to ac-
commodate the expectations of the dominant group of white
males. The very fact of having to adopt different modes of behavior for different audiences introduces an element of complexity and potential conflict to the lives of those who are

most caught up in a marginal existence. House slaves, for example, faced the inordinately difficult dilemma of being part of an oppressed group of slaves even as they lived in intimacy with and under the constant surveillance of the white master-class, thereby experiencing in its most extreme form the conflict of living in two worlds.[41]

Ordinarily, the tension implicit in such a situation is deflected, or as Richard Wright observed, "contained and controlled by reflex." Most house slaves seemed to learn how to live with the conflict by repressing their anger and uneasiness. Coping with the situation became a matter of instinct. But it is not surprising that many slave revolts were led by those house slaves who could not resolve the conflict by reflex, and instead were driven to alienation and protest. For the minority of people who misinterpreted the cues given them or learned too late how to cope, consciousness of the conflict made instinctive conformity impossible. As Richard Wright observed, "I could not make subservience an automatic part of my behavior. . . . while standing before a white man . . . I had to figure out how to say each word . . . I could not grin . . . I could not react as the world in which I lived expected me to." The pain of self-consciousness made the burden almost unbearable. As Maya Angelou has written, awareness of displacement "is the rust on the razor that threatens the throat." In an endless string of injuries, it was the final insult.[42]

Dissenting blacks and women have shared this experience of being "the outsider." Unable to accept the stereotyped behavior prescribed for their group, they have, in Vivian Gornick's words, "stood beyond the embrace of their fellows." With acute vision, Gornick writes, the outsider is able to "see deeply into the circle, penetrating to its very center, his vision a needle piercing the heart of life. Invariably, what he sees is intolerable." On the basis of such a vision, exile is the only alternative available. Yet, ironically, it too serves to reinforce the status quo by removing from the situation those most likely to fight it. Until the numbers willing to resist become great enough, the system of social control remains unaltered.[43]

It seems fair to conclude, therefore, that a significant resemblance has existed in the forms of social control used to
keep women and blacks in their "place." Despite profound
substantive differences between women and blacks, and white
women and black women, all have been victims of a process,
the end product of which has been to take away the power to
define one's own aspirations, destiny, and sense of self. In each
case a relationship of subservience to the dominant group has
been perpetuated by physical, economic, psychological, and
internal controls that have functioned in a remarkably similar
way to discourage deviancy and place a premium on conformity. "It was brutal to be Negro and have no control over
my life," Maya Angelou observes in her autobiography. "It
was brutal to be young and already trained to sit quietly."
From a feminist perspective, the same words describe the
process of control experienced by most women.[44]

The core of this process has been the use of a visible, physical characteristic as the basis for assigning to each group a
network of duties, responsibilities, and attributes. It is the
physical foundation for discriminatory treatment which
makes the process of social control on sex and race distinctive
from that which has applied to other oppressed groups. Class,
for example, comes closest to sex and race as a source of massive social inequity and injustice. Yet in an American context, class has been difficult to isolate as an organizing principle. Because class is not associated with a visible physical
characteristic and many working class people persist in identifying with a middle-class life-style, class is not a category
easy to identify in terms of physical or psychological control.
(The very tendency to abjure class consciousness in favor of a
social mobility ethic, of course, is its own form of psychological control.) Ethnicity too has frequently served as a basis
for oppression, but the ease with which members of most
ethnic minorities have been able to "pass" into the dominant
culture has made the structure of social control in those cases
both porous and complicated. Thus although in almost every
instance invidious treatment has involved the use of some
form of physical, economic, psychological, or internal con-

trols, the combinations have been different and the exceptions frequent.

The analogy of sex and race is distinctive, therefore, precisely to the extent that it highlights in pure form the process of social control which has operated to maintain the existing structure of American society. While many have been victimized by the same types of control, only in the case of sex and race—where physical attributes are ineradicable—have these controls functioned systematically and clearly to define from birth the possibilities to which members of a group might aspire. Perhaps for that reason sex and race have been cornerstones of the social system, and the source of values and attitudes which have both reinforced the power of the dominant class and provided a weapon for dividing potential opposition.

Finally, the analogy provides a potential insight into the strategies and possibilities of social change. If women and blacks have been kept in their "place" by similar forms of social control, the prerequisites for liberation may consist of overcoming those forms of social control through a similar process. In the case of both women and blacks, the fundamental problem has been that others have controlled the power to define one's existence. Thus, to whatever extent women and blacks act or think in a given way solely because of the expectation of the dominant group rather than from their own choice, they remain captive to the prevailing system of social control. The prototypical American woman, writes Vivian Gornick, is perceived as "never taking, always being taken, never absorbed by her own desire, preoccupied only with whether or not she is desired." Within such a context, the "other" is always more important than the "self" in determining one's sense of individual identity. It is for this reason that efforts by blacks and women toward group solidarity, control over one's own institutions, and development of an autonomous and positive self-image may be crucial in breaking the bonds of external dominance.[45]

Yet such a change itself depends on development of a collective consciousness of oppression and a collective commitment to protest. As long as social and political conditions, or the reluctance of group members to participate, preclude the emergence of group action, the individual rebel has little chance of effecting change. Thus the issue of social control leads inevitably to the question of how the existing cycle is broken. What are the preconditions for the evolution of group protest? How do external influences stimulate, or forestall, the will to resist? And through what modes of organization and action does the struggle for autonomy proceed? For these questions too, the analogy of sex and race may provide a useful frame of reference.

Whatever the case, it seems more productive to focus on forms of control or processes of change than to dwell on the substantive question of whether blacks and women have suffered comparable physical and material injury. Clearly, they have not. On the other hand when two groups exist in a situation of inequality, it may be self-defeating to become embroiled in a quarrel over which is more unequal or the victim of greater oppression. The more salient question is how a condition of inequality for both is maintained and perpetuated—through what modes is it reinforced? By that criterion, continued exploration of the analogy of sex and race promises to bring added insight to the study of how American society operates.

IV.

The Analogy of Social Change

During the 1960's no movements for social change threatened the established order more than the drives for racial equality and women's liberation. Each drew upon sacred ideals from the American creed, yet neither was content to stay within the reform traditions of the past. Instead, the two movements carved out new grounds of social protest, assaulted some of the most entrenched cultural assumptions of the nation, and sought to alter living patterns fundamental to the perpetuation of the social structure as it had existed. For that reason alone, a connection between the two movements is warranted. But the deeper significance of the analogy lies in the extent to which change on the issues of sex and race emerged through a similar process and passed through comparable stages of development. The purpose of this chapter is to explore that process.

Before turning to the experience of blacks and women respectively, it may be useful to look again at some of the problems of definition raised in the first two chapters. One of the distinctions crucial to this chapter is that between social change and collective protest. During the turmoil of the 1960's the two frequently became confused because any discussion of social change seemed automatically to entail aligning oneself for or against the demands of a particular social protest group. Yet as the example of the industrial revolution makes clear, the lives of millions of people can be altered decisively by external forces which, initially at least, seem independent of pursuit of a particular goal by a particular group.

On the other hand, social change from whatever source generally gives rise to collective behavior. Industrial capitalists seized upon the technological innovations of the 19th century to consolidate power. Workers, in turn, sought to protect their interests but fared less well because of the absence of legal, financial, and political strength. Still other groups organized to promote social reform. Their successes, such as enactment of the Prohibition amendment and the winning of woman's suffrage, illustrate the convergence of social change and social activism, where the change that occurs results directly from the organized activity of a particular group.[1]

The basic problem, then, is to determine the relation of social change to specific collective behavior, attempting where possible to pinpoint causal connections. In explaining social change, especially involving oppressed groups, there have been two general patterns. Within the first, external forces are perceived as largely responsible for whatever progress or decline a given group experiences. At its extreme, such a position minimizes, or discounts entirely, the possibility of people affecting their own destinies. Thus, for example, it has been argued that changes in the lives of black Americans during the 1960's resulted primarily from external economic circumstances and the social policies of white liberals, with blacks themselves playing only a minor role. The second position, by contrast, perceives change as emanating solely from the organized activity of people seeking to gain control of their own lives. In this second view, black Americans never were internally affected by external structures of control, and the changes of the 1960's represented a triumph of generations of protest. Clearly, neither of these positions adequately addresses the complexity of the links between impersonal processes of change and self-initiated collective activity, but they highlight how important is the chemistry of the interaction—a chemistry which conceivably differs for each situation and group.

This, in turn, raises the issue of what each group brings to the process of change. Is it necessary, for example, for social and economic conditions to reach a certain point before protest develops? Does a sense of oppression exist as a constant among those who are discriminated against, or does it emerge only under special circumstances? And what is the connection between individual expression of protest or discontent and the development of collective activity? * Here, of course, the substantive differences between women and blacks are crucial. The collective physical, economic, and psychological discrimination experienced by Afro-Americans almost ensures a universal awareness of oppression and commitment to change. In this sense, group awareness would be constant, while external conditions—one's environment, the political climate, the economy—would be significant in determining how much, and what kind of change one could envision. The diverse social and economic existence experienced by women, in contrast, discourages the same degree of collective awareness, giving rise to differing perceptions of the need for change. Although few blacks have anything to lose from a change in race relations, many women benefit from the status quo of sex relations and would have to sacrifice material, as well as psychological, assets were the existing distribution of sex roles altered. In the particular dynamics of each group's

---

* In the case of both women and blacks there is ample historical evidence of discontent. As we have seen, black Americans found ways of expressing protest even under the most stringent forms of social control. Whether in the lyrics of slave spirituals crying out for freedom, the frequent occurrences of slave runaways from plantations, the development of black political organizations after emancipation, or the lengthy history of verbal protest within black communities, the historical record indicates continuing awareness of oppression and desire for change among Afro-Americans. In the case of women, expressions of discontent have been more muted, but sufficient to prove significant dissatisfaction with the status quo. Not only have there been the women's rights and suffrage movements, but as Carroll Smith-Rosenberg has shown, some women expressed their frustration through hysteria and neurasthenia. Probably the most dramatic evidence of female discontent in the 20th century (prior to the 1960's) was found in a 1947 Roper poll which showed that 25 per cent of all women wished they had been born men rather than women. Had such alienation been discovered among men (it was not), it would have been taken as indisputable proof of a major rebellion against one's social condition. Still, there remains the problem of distinguishing overt collective behavior from individual or covert expressions of anger.[2]

response to generalized social change, then, women and blacks bring significantly different contributions to the equation.

With these qualifications acknowledged, it may be possible to analyze more clearly the process of social change on the issues of sex and race. The key questions concern the impact of external forces on social and economic circumstances, the relationship of norms to behavior, and the collective sense of self which different groups developed, especially in terms of awareness and self-perception. A look at the experience first of Afro-Americans, then of women, in the years after 1940 provides a basis for comparison.

Until the beginning of World War II, a combination of economic, political, and social intimidation successfully undercut the possibility of a concerted drive among black Americans for racial equality. Although protest organizations such as the NAACP worked effectively within the court system for legal change, the vast majority of black people lived in circumstances that precluded social protest. Three out of four blacks lived in the South, where the crop lien system operated to keep both white and black tenant farmers in a state of perpetual economic bondage. A pervasive etiquette of race, reinforced wherever necessary by terrorism, prevented even minor challenges to the status quo. During the New Deal a number of Roosevelt Administration officials supported changes to help blacks, including fair allocation of relief money in many places and a larger recognition of blacks in political appointments. Still, the first to suffer from the Depression had been those at the bottom, and even the supposedly friendly Roosevelt Administration failed to put its weight behind legislation to abolish lynching or outlaw the poll tax. At the end of the 1930's the masses of black people were still oppressed, politically and economically, and protest organizations voiced anger at the failure of New Deal leaders to act on even the most clear-cut issues of civil rights.[3]

World War II brought a significant departure from past patterns—in the behavior of blacks if not in the dominant culture's attitudes. The urgency of meeting the defense crisis made it imperative for the government to recruit into industry and the armed forces millions of people who previously had been excluded from significant positions in society. Black leaders, recognizing an unparalleled opportunity, used the lever of the crisis to drive home a series of demands for reform which, if put into effect, would bring greater civil rights for blacks in return for loyal support of the war effort. The most notable example of this strategy was the March on Washington Movement (MOW) led by labor organizer A. Philip Randolph in 1941. Threatening to bring as many as 50,000 black protestors to Washington in the midst of Congressional debate on military preparedness bills, Randolph and his coalition of black leaders successfully extracted from the Administration a pledge to secure equal opportunity for blacks in all defense-related industries. The MOW Movement, composed exclusively of blacks, represented a daring departure and forced the national Administration to acknowledge, at least formally, black complaints.[4]

On a deeper level, however, the war itself proved more decisive to the long-term history of change in race relations. By causing a massive dislocation of population and forcing millions of people into new experiences, the war created a context in which some people both perceived and responded to the issue of race in a different way. The vicious cycle of social control which had compelled obedience to traditional patterns as the price for survival was at least partially broken by the massive jolt of full-scale war. Although little was accomplished in the way of permanent progress toward equality, the changes which did occur laid the foundations for the development of mass protest activity in subsequent years.

The first great impact of the war was an accelerated migration of blacks from the South, and within the South from farm to city. Whether lured by a specific job in a munitions plant, ordered by a directive from the Selective Service, or simply beckoned by the prospect of a better life elsewhere, millions of black Southerners boarded trains and buses and headed north and west. When they arrived at their destinations, they frequently found living situations less attractive than they had expected. The urban ghetto, with its overcrowded housing, hard-pressed social facilities, and oppressive discrimination, seemed to many not much better than what they had left behind. Yet there was a difference as well. The Northern urban political machine sought votes and offered some political recognition in return. The community was new, the imminent tyranny of small-town authorities was removed, and psychological freedom was greater. The very act of physical mobility brought independence from the overwhelming constraints of social control in small Southern communities. If the controls existed in different forms in the new community, there was at least the possibility of different perspectives and a heightened sense of what might be done to achieve a better life.

The second major effect of the war was a limited amount of economic mobility. The lure of jobs in the North and in urban areas of the South was not totally without substance. Some 2,000,000 blacks were employed in defense plants during the war and another 200,000 joined the federal civil service. Most of these jobs were at low levels. Blacks continued to be hired as janitors or as scrub-women rather than as technicians or secretaries. Still, as the war progressed, there was more chance of better positions. In 1940 the number of blacks employed in professional, white-collar, skilled or semi-skilled jobs had been less than 20 per cent. A decade later the figure had climbed to 33 per cent, largely as a result of wartime changes. The number of blacks in labor unions doubled to 1,250,000 during the war years. The end result was thus a confused picture: enough upward mobility had occurred to spur hope, but constant discrimination reinforced a sense of how much needed to be done.

The third great impact came in the armed forces. When the war began, blacks protested vigorously that they were not drafted in proportion to their numbers in the population. They insisted on being trained alongside whites and given the same opportunity to fight in combat units. Although some progress occurred on these issues, persistent maltreatment of black soldiers made a mockery of the government's claim to be fighting a war against racism. While President Roosevelt repeatedly told the world that the country was fighting for freedom and democracy, training camps were torn by prejudice and discrimination, Red Cross blood supplies were segregated into "white" and "colored," and blacks frequently were the victims of violence from whites in local communities where they were stationed.[5]

Significantly, each of the major shifts initiated by World War II exhibited a common theme: the interaction of some change for the better with pervasive reminders of ongoing racism. The chemistry of the process was crucial. At the same time that new exposure to travel, jobs, and higher expectations exerted an emancipating effect on people's perception of the world, day-to-day contact with discrimination in the armed forces, poor housing in the urban ghetto, and blatant prejudice on the job had an embittering effect. The juxtaposition could not help but spawn anger and frustration. The experience of some improvement generated the expectation for still more, and, when those expectations were dashed, a rising tide of frustration and protest resulted.

In this sense, the experience of black Americans during World War II provided a paradigm for race relations over the ensuing three decades. The major theme of black history from the 40's through the 70's has been of promises made and then betrayed, creating a framework for ever growing disillusionment among blacks and an increasing insistence among them on direct action to secure their rights.

The promise of effective progress on civil rights through a biracial coalition of liberals took specific form in the mid-40's. During the war itself, crowded living conditions, racial conflict over jobs, and the resentment of angry whites led to numerous race riots. The frightening example of racial turmoil caused many white leaders to pledge support for change in race relations. During the Truman Administration especially, the record of verbal support for civil rights seemed strong. Truman appointed a special Committee on Civil Rights with enough liberals on it to guarantee that the subsequent report would spell out in detail the measures needed to correct discrimination. Truman enthusiastically endorsed the report early in 1948 and later became the first President to take his political campaign to Harlem. The subsequent outpouring of black votes for Truman—the margin of victory in some states—caused many observers to see the President's statements on civil rights as the key to his re-election.

Verbal support rarely translated into action, however. Fearful of alienating his political constituency in the white South, Truman never pushed hard for implementation of his civil rights recommendations, nor did he take decisive executive action to deliver on the promises he had made. Although the order to desegregate the armed forces was issued in 1948, the majority of military units remained segregated until after the Korean War. From the perspective of the President, of course, more had been done to legitimize the issue of civil rights and educate the public than ever before. But from the point of view of many blacks, the words had accomplished little for the people being talked about. Truman's symbolic political action during the campaign had continued to encourage hope, but when it came to substance, the record was skimpy.[6]

In some ways the most decisive embodiment of the theme of promise and betrayal came with the Supreme Court's 1954 ruling in *Brown v. Board of Education* declaring that segregated schools were unconstitutional. The black press responded to the decision with universal acclaim, voicing the conviction of most black people that the Court's action meant an end forthwith to all the evils of segregation. Much of the white press expressed the same expectation of rapid change, and even some Southern governors appeared resigned to major shifts. Yet the practical response once again fell drastically short of the mark. President Eisenhower consistently refused to lend moral support for the decision; the courts themselves backed off from requiring immediate enforcement; and almost every Southern state—tacitly encouraged by Washington's inaction—successfully avoided even minimal steps toward desegregation.[7]

Bitter disappointment over the failure to enforce the *Brown* decision took place in the context of continued frustration in other areas as well. The fact that black people remained poor at a time when the rest of the nation seemed to be making giant strides toward affluence only accentuated discontent. In 1959 a black college graduate could expect to earn in a lifetime less than a white person with an eighth grade education. Nearly half of all black citizens fell below the poverty line. While blacks watched the same tantalizing television ads as whites and shared the same desire for a decent house and adequate schooling for their children, they were consistently denied the chance to acquire good housing or hold the jobs which would give them access to the "affluent" society.[8]

It was against this background of rising expectations and continuing disillusionment that black Americans took matters into their own hands. The emergence of the modern civil rights movement can be traced to the December day in 1955 when Rosa Parks refused to move to the back of a Montgomery bus and was arrested as a result. The next day the black community of Montgomery responded with a total boycott of the city's bus lines. The year-long siege that followed was notable for three primary reasons: first, it showed that virtually 100 per cent of the black population was willing to stand up for its rights regardless of intimidation, thereby shattering the tired cliché that local blacks were satisfied; second, it illustrated the way in which a movement once under way generates its own momentum and vision, as the boycott committee's demands changed from greater courtesy toward blacks within a segregated bus system to a demand for complete desegregation of the buses; and third, it brought to the fore a young black minister who preached a philosophy of non-violent resistance as a means of overcoming racial injustice. Under Martin Luther King Jr.'s leadership, the church—the foremost institution within the black community and in the past freqently an instrument of social control—became at once the center of a mass movement for social change. Four years later, the same spirit that had motivated the Montgomery movement led black students in Greensboro, North Carolina, to sit in at the local Woolworth's lunch counter and demand equal service. Within days, their example was emulated by other black students throughout the South, as sit-ins erupted in nearly every state below the Mason-Dixon line. As one demonstration led to another, protest became a national by-word, and the era of modern-day social activism was begun.[9]

Even in the halcyon days of the civil rights movement, however, the theme of promises betrayed continued to shape the history of race relations. Although white students from the North and some from the South joined blacks in sit-ins and kneel-ins and pray-ins, politicians in Washington failed to respond with decisive actions. John F. Kennedy promised to sign an executive order barring discrimination in federally financed housing, then waited two years before putting pen to paper. The Justice Department pledged protection for travelers seeking to desegregate interstate buses and for voter registration workers, but in far too many cases FBI agents stood by as local white sheriffs beat up peaceful demonstrators. In addition, the conquest of some barriers to equality simply disclosed the presence of others, and as more and more young people joined the movement, impatience over government inaction outpaced the slow rate of progress. As civil rights leaders pointed out, it was one thing to have the right to eat at the Holiday Inn and another to have the money to buy decent food. As the problem of racism was probed deeper and deeper, confidence in the willingness of the government to respond adequately diminished even further.

Tensions within the movement itself highlighted the ongoing conflict over the value of looking to whites for support. Martin Luther King, Jr., headed an informal national coalition of church leaders, labor representatives, liberal politicians, Northern white financial supporters, and blacks. The fact that he was forced to be responsive to all elements of the coalition in order to achieve his legislative goals irritated younger and more radical activists. From the perspective of some members of the Student Non-violent Coordinating Committee (SNCC), it sometimes seemed that King cared more about cultivating the media and his Northern liberal constituency than about blacks working in the rural counties of Alabama, Georgia, and Mississippi. To young militants the white establishment had done nothing to earn consideration from the civil rights movement. When the March on Washington took place in the summer of 1963, influential white liberals had urged SNCC leader John Lewis to tone down his speech because it was too radical. And when the Mississippi Freedom Democratic Party went to the Democratic National Convention in 1964 with damning evidence of fraud and intimidation on the part of Mississippi's white Democrats, it was Northern white liberals who were responsible for forcing through a compromise which gave blacks only two seats instead of the twenty they sought and could have won.[10]

As a result there developed within the movement itself a growing demand for blacks to be in complete control, even if that meant the exclusion of whites. The slogan "black and white together" had appealed to the deepest idealism of many young Americans, white and black, who wished to eliminate the tensions born of centuries of racism and create a "beloved community." But to many members of SNCC, working with whites became synonymous with continued paternalism and white domination. Black leaders like Stokely Carmichael and Rap Brown asked whether integration was not, in its own way, another form of subjugation, with blacks accepting white norms, white habits, and white souls. If integration meant assimilation, what would happen to the black past, the distinctive characteristics of black culture, and above all the right of black people to define and carve out their own destiny?

It was within the context of these tensions that the issue of racial pride and identity came to the fore in the summer of 1966 with Stokely Carmichael's call for "Black Power." Quickly the new slogan came to symbolize the determination of blacks to define themselves and control their own communities. Coinciding with the growing interest in African dress, hairstyles, language, and culture, the phrase "Black Power" represented a conscious proclamation that many blacks were no longer willing to accept white promises or white standards. In the years prior to the 1960's blacks had been petitioners, seeking their rights within the established order and appealing to the historic American Creed of equal opportu-

nity and brotherhood. The Negro Dream, Martin Luther
King, Jr., had said in the 1963 March on Washington, was
rooted "in the American dream." Now many blacks were
demanding instead of petitioning, and stating to the wider
society that they would determine the scope of their own destiny. Whatever the final consequences of the shift in strategy
and symbols, it was clear that a new era had dawned. No
longer would many blacks accept the definition of their
place—psychological, political or economic—as dictated by
whites. No longer would they subscribe to the "rules of the
game" established by the dominant culture—at least not
unless they chose to do so.[11]

For women as well, the period beginning in 1940 marked
a time of change. Although enactment of the Nineteenth
Amendment represented an important achievement on the
road to equality, it did not, as we have seen, generate significant change in how sex roles were defined and allocated.
Overt discrimination, together with traditional patterns of
socialization, combined to discourage most women from de-
parting from their prescribed sphere. There were few role
models to emulate, little possibility of social approval, and
the pervasive pressure of the culture to marry and conform to
the ideal of homemaker. In such a situation most women did
not question the boundaries set for them by their parents,
peers, and schools.

World War II provided the occasion for at least a tempo-
rary change in this pattern. The desperate need for workers
to produce munitions as well as take the jobs of men gone off
to fight led to a massive public relations campaign designed
to recruit women into the labor force. "YOU'RE GOING
TO EMPLOY WOMEN," a War Department pamphlet
stated. Almost overnight, the labor force was transformed by
an influx of female workers. In one California aircraft plant,
13,000 men and no women had been employed in the fall of
1941. A year later there were 13,000 women and 11,000
men. More than six and a half million women joined the
work force in the four years of war, a 57 per cent increase in
the number of women workers. Women performed almost

every job imaginable, from running huge cranes to repairing aircraft engines to driving taxi cabs. More important, most of the workers came from the home and previously had been occupied exclusively as homemakers. Nearly 75 per cent of the new workers were married, and 60 per cent were over thirty-five.

Despite these vast statistical changes, however, little progress took place on issues of equality between the sexes. The National War Labor Board issued orders calling for equal pay for equal work, but the government's anti-inflation policy, together with loopholes in the directive, made it possible for most employers to continue discriminating in the wages they paid men and women simply by changing job labels from "female" to "worker-trainee." Women for the most part were excluded from major policy-making decisions within business and government. In addition, public officials were slow to respond to the urgent need for community services to help women workers. This was particularly true in the case of day-care centers. Absenteeism in order to take care of children was a primary cause of lost work hours among women, yet until the last eighteen months of the war little was done to provide public facilities to deal with the problem.

Although government agencies like the Labor Department's Women's Bureau and private organizations such as the National Business and Professional Women's Clubs pressed for greater government action, the vast majority of women workers did not engage in militant protest about their working conditions or subscribe to any feminist cause. Most came to work in the first place out of patriotism or a desire to keep the family together economically in the midst of wartime. Most found that they enjoyed their work, welcomed the challenge, were grateful for the camaraderie of fellow workers, and could use the money. At the same time there was little evidence of feminist consciousness or commitment to the notion of equal rights and opportunities between the sexes. Wages were higher than before, better jobs were available, and concerted protest was minimal.[12]

Nevertheless, expectations among women about their own social and economic roles changed drastically during the war.

93

In 1942 very few of those women who took jobs indicated
that they planned to stay once the fighting was over. A return to home and children seemed nearly a universal expectation. By 1945, in contrast, approximately 75 to 80 per cent
of women war workers indicated that they intended, or at
least desired, to remain on the job. Such women enjoyed the
social and economic advantages of working and saw no reason
why they should give up their positions. As one worker commented, "War jobs have uncovered unsuspected abilities in
American women. Why lose all these abilities because of a
belief that a woman's place is in the home. For some it is, for
others not." [13]

Within this context, the major theme in the experience of
women during the postwar years was a gap between the behavior of women in the labor force and the resurgence of
traditional attitudes toward woman's "place" in the home.
Almost immediately after the war ended, a concerted campaign developed among political leaders, the media, and employers to persuade women to return to the home. The war
had been an unsettling experience, uprooting millions of people from home and family. Since women were seen as the
anchor of the family, it seemed to many observers imperative
that they return to the home lest the entire society be thrown
out of kilter. As one sociologist wrote, "Women must bear
and rear children. Husbands must support them." Throughout the late 1940's and 1950's, what Betty Friedan would
later call the "feminine mystique" became a ubiquitous force
in the popular culture. Any mother who worked, one psychi-
atrist wrote, was "stimulated by neurotic competition." Mag-
azines featured spreads of three- and four-children families,
praised women who became professionals at homemaking,
and glorified family togetherness.

Even as the campaign to bring women back to the kitchen
flourished, however, the percentage of women in the labor
force continued to spiral. Inflation, a rising standard of living, and the desire to share the benefits of consumerism all
encouraged the growth of the two-income family. In the
1950's women in the labor force were increasing at a rate four
times faster than men, and by 1960 40 per cent of all women

over sixteen were in the labor force compared with 25 per
cent in 1940. More important, most of the new workers were
married and many had young children. By the end of the
1960's nearly 45 per cent of all married women were employed compared with 15 per cent in 1940, and the figure included more than half of all mothers with children aged six
to seventeen. Ironically, the same women who were described
in the *Ladies' Home Journal* and *McCall's* as thriving on housework were spending an increasing amount of their time in
gainful employment. The contradiction between cultural
norms and actual behavior could hardly have been more pronounced.[14]

Still, most women appeared able to live with the contradiction, or at least were not sufficiently disturbed by it to
challenge traditional attitudes. Throughout most of the late
1940's and 1950's, feminism remained a marginal movement
with little popular support. Popular attitudes were reflected
in a Women's Bureau memorandum, which described feminists as "a small but militant group of leisure class women
[giving vent] to their resentment at not having been born
men." Most women workers had not taken their jobs out of a
desire to compete with men but rather to help the family—a
traditional role—so that children could go to college, a new
addition could be built on the house, or the family could
have a longer and better vacation. The vast majority of female
workers were employed in traditional "woman's work,"
which featured almost total occupational segregation and little if any possibility of upward mobility. In short, women had
expanded their sphere outside of the home, but without altering either the assumptions about their "place" or the actual
pattern of discrimination which kept them in sex-typed jobs.
To work was one thing; to call into question traditional attitudes toward sex roles was another. For the latter to happen,
new perceptions had to evolve and a new frame of reference
had to develop.[15]

If feminist consciousness itself was slow to develop, however, a process of change was under way which helped prepare
the ground for action later on. The very fact of massive
increases in female employment destroyed the reality of tradi-

95

tional notions of woman's "place" in the home. No longer did conventional stereotypes correspond to women's experience. Moreover, some changes within the family occurred as a result of women's employment. Children of parents who both worked grew up with substantially different ideas of what was permissible for men and women to do. Daughters of working mothers indicated that they, too, planned to work after marriage, and numerous studies showed that young girls were more likely to name their mother as the person they most admired if she worked than if she did not work. None of these changes signified progress toward equality, but they did help provide a basis for a challenge to traditional attitudes.[16]

The event which more than any other crystallized a sense of grievance among later women activists was the emergence of the civil rights movement. Because women did not live together in a ghetto or share a common political and economic experience on a continuing basis, they had tended to view their problems as individual rather than social. As Betty Friedan observed in *The Feminine Mystique,* many discontented women talked about "a problem that has no name," convinced that their own unhappiness was something personal. The civil rights movement, however, focused attention on the extent to which groups of people were oppressed on the basis of cultural and physical characteristics. As women saw and participated in demonstrations demanding freedom and personal dignity, they perceived, like their abolitionist forerunners, a connection to their own lives and hence the possibility of acting for themselves as a group.

The civil rights movement proved significant on one level as a model for political activity and a vehicle for legislative reform. When the 1964 Civil Rights Act was passed, Title VII included a ban on discrimination in employment on the basis of sex as well as race. Older women activists—particularly business and professional women, and veterans of national and state Commissions on the Status of Women—seized on Title VII as an instrument for change. When the government failed to act on complaints of sex discrimination, these activists formed the National Organization of Women

(NOW) in 1966 to mobilize pressure on behalf of women's rights. Other groups quickly followed. The Women's Equity Action League organized in 1970 to press court actions for women's civil rights, and in one of the most notable events of the legal battle, instituted a class action complaint against every university in the country for the practice of sex discrimination. The National Women's Political Caucus, in turn, developed to push the nation's political parties toward recognition of women's rights. At each step along the way, black organizations and political strategy provided a model.

Just as important, the civil rights movement itself spurred younger women participants to take action against the discrimination which they experienced from their colleagues in the movement. Repeatedly, young women in SNCC (and later SDS) found that they were either excluded from policy-making positions or treated as servants. On the basis of heightened consciousness about sex discrimination in their own immediate lives, as well as participation in a movement designed to eliminate inequality wherever it existed, young women in the movement organized themselves to seek change. Mobilized into action by personal experience, they took the organizing skills and ideological lessons which they had learned in the civil rights movement and became the initiators of the women's liberation movement. Together with the founders of NOW and the discontented middle-class women who had been galvanized by the message of Betty Friedan, these young women provided the core around which a revived woman's movement developed.

The principal organizing tactic of the new feminism was the "consciousness raising" session where women gathered to reveal and discuss in a supportive atmosphere the problems they had encountered on the basis of their sex. Such sessions provided the energy for the entire movement, transforming the perceptions of the participants about their own lives and leading to activity designed to overcome discrimination. As movement women talked about their experiences and came to the realization that they shared a common grievance, they also grew in the conviction that their grievances could be redressed only by acting together.[17]

The consciousness raising session addressed a primary obstacle to political effectiveness: the lack of sex solidarity. If women were to wage an effective struggle, it was reasoned, they needed to forge bonds of togetherness that would transcend their isolation in individual families and foster the same sense of collective experience which blacks or Chicanos derived from living together in a ghetto. A community of support was needed, and the women's liberation group provided such a community for its members. Though a wife might be unable to express dissatisfaction to her husband on her own, the existence of an intimate circle of associates sharing a common purpose offered reinforcement and an incentive for action. Similarly, community institutions such as schools and hospitals were likely to prove more responsive to the organized effort of a woman's group than to the request of a single individual. The consciousness raising group thus served as a departure point for the principal strategy of women's liberation: to use sex solidarity as a means of breaking down sex barriers and sex stereotypes.

By 1970 the woman's movement had itself become a major force for change within the society. Treated as a joke by some, it provoked profound and energetic resistance from others. Yet the drive for new attitudes and new patterns of behavior continued and grew. A legal suit which described the American Telephone and Telegraph Company as "the largest oppressor of women workers in the United States" produced an out of court settlement of back pay to women workers and more important, a plan to change hiring and promotion practices so that men would be placed in formerly all "female" jobs and women would be assigned to previously all "male" positions. Charges of discrimination within colleges and universities led to government investigation, and an order for educational institutions to provide affirmative action plans for hiring and promoting women and blacks. And women in politics secured the pledge of major parties and candidates to guarantee women an important voice in party councils. The biggest change of all, however, was the fact that a growing minority of women insisted on finding a new definition of their identity—one which would no longer rely on cultural preconceptions of masculinity and femininity. In so doing, they rejected the cultural norms of the past and attempted to create new ground rules for relations between the sexes in the future.

Clearly, important differences separate the experience of blacks and women during the last three decades. To begin with, blacks exhibited a much greater readiness to protest than women. A full-scale civil rights movement emerged in the black population by the end of the 1950's and would have been supported prior to that time had the context been right. In contrast, it took until the late 1960's before a strong women's movement developed. Similarly, it would be foolish to underestimate the conflicts which have existed between women and blacks. As we have seen, black men and most black women have viewed the women's movement as a diversionary struggle that constitutes a potential threat to the primary goal of racial freedom and strength. On the other side, many white women have shown indifference, or at least insensitivity, to the issue of racism.

Nevertheless, the parallels that emerge from comparing the two case studies are striking, particularly if one looks at the components contributing to change. The similarity lies not in the substantive identity of female and black response (although there were substantive connections), but in the process by which change occurred, and the progression of both groups through comparable layers of change, culminating in a remarkably similar effort by black and female activists to define their own goals and identity. Thus, despite the disparity of experience in the two groups, similar variables have been involved in the process of change through which each moved.

The first parallel consists of the impact of World War II on the status quo as it existed for both groups. The war intervened in the prevailing pattern of daily life to create what the sociologist Neil Smelser has called the "structural conduciveness" for change.* Indeed, it took an event of the magnitude of world war to disrupt the cycle of economic, politi-

---

* The following analysis draws frequently on the ideas developed by Neil Smelser in his *Theory of Collective Behavior,* (New York, 1965), but it is not based exclusively on Smelser's model.

cal, psychological, and internal controls that previously had maintained women and blacks in their assigned "place." World War II accomplished this by reordering, for the moment at least, the priorities of the society, making possible the entry of women and blacks into roles and activities hitherto considered inappropriate. Like an electric shock, the war jarred the social system and prompted a rearranging of roles, perceptions, and responsibilities.

Significantly, the war crisis called forth character traits radically different from those that had been emphasized before, thereby helping to pave the way for longer lasting change. As a result of the manpower emergency, the government and other institutions encouraged people who previously had been taught to be docile—i.e. "well adjusted" to their condition—to become instead aggressive, self-sufficient, and confident. Those who had been warned to stay in their place now were told it was a matter of patriotic duty to leave that place and assert themselves in new roles. The war thus placed a premium on personality attributes most psychologists would view as healthy (even if deviant by previous standards), as opposed to a pattern of pathological adjustment to a situation of discrimination. In short, for the first time in the lives of many people character traits necessary to freedom and independence were encouraged; once given the possibility for expression, it was not likely such attributes would quickly disappear.

The second major parallel was a pattern of glaring contradiction between norms and reality that developed for both groups after the war. The nature of the contradictions differed significantly for blacks as opposed to women. In the one instance, norms of equality and non-discrimination received an infusion of vitality during and after World War II, and the contradiction consisted of a failure by the government and others to enforce the renewed verbal commitment to equality and justice. The disparity between promise and reality helped to accentuate black anger and frustration. In the case of women, on the other hand, norms remained constant, while behavior deviated more and more from traditional ideas. The central concept of the "feminine mystique"—the all-consuming glory of domesticity—was at odds with the rapidly rising number of women who were employed and who seemed to enjoy working outside the home.

Regardless of the nature of the contradiction, the core point was the significance of such stress for social change. Traditional cultural norms remain unchallenged as long as people's behavior is perceived as either consistent with the norms or irrelevant to them. Thus when the "place" of most American women was in fact in the home, there was no frame of reference in reality from which to attack the conventional norm. Conversely, as long as the values of equal opportunity and justice were not viewed as applicable to blacks, there was little basis for the dominant culture to support civil rights activity. The emergence of glaring inconsistencies, in contrast, highlights the presence of a problem requiring action. In the case of both women and blacks, the existence of contradictions between norms and behavior in the postwar period did not automatically mean the start of a collective protest movement; but building upon the changes of World War II, the contradictions provided one more ingredient to the foundation necessary for social movements to develop.[18]

The third element common to the process of change was the presence of a catalyst that galvanized already existing elements and helped forge them into a social movement. The role of a catalyst, or a "precipitating event" as Smelser calls it, is to provide the final connection that in turn brings different ingredients together and transforms what was previously diffuse and passive into something focused and active. The catalytic event is not itself sufficient to generate collective behavior, but it is the indispensable factor that helps give form and direction to the otherwise unrelated components of change.

In the case of the civil rights movement, the 1954 *Brown* decision and the failure to implement it provided such a catalyst. The *Brown* decision itself, of course, represented in its purest form the promise of equal rights which had been held forth to black Americans. The aftermath, in turn, exemplified, in stark terms, the gap between promise and performance. In the face of such high expectations, the absence of any meaningful progress spurred the direct action which took place, first in Montgomery, then throughout the South. The convergence of hope and disillusionment around a simple yet powerfully symbolic event brought energy and focus to civil rights protest.

In a similar fashion, the civil rights movement itself served as a catalytic event for the women's movement. Up until the early 1960's, those who had consistently advocated a feminist position, or suggested in less explicit ways the need for a change in women's status, had been unable to find a vehicle to communicate their message, or a way to connect their views to the existing social environment. The civil rights movement both provided a dramatic example of the point which women activists were trying to communicate, and it provided a model of protest which helped bring a women's movement to life. It thereby gave women a profoundly political picture of their society and underlined the significance of sex consciousness as an organizing principle. Just as the *Brown* decision had crystallized the issue of protest for blacks, the civil rights movement illustrated with unmistakable clarity to women the possibility of people uniting on the basis of sex identity to preserve their dignity and secure equal treatment.

The fourth common element was the development of an innovative tactic which in the case of both women and blacks served as a rallying point for activists and a symbol of protest. In the postwar history of race relations, the discovery of the sit-in tactic by four black college students in Greensboro, North Carolina, provided such a rallying point. The nonviolent sit-ins served an astonishing variety of purposes: they gave blacks an opportunity to assert their rights in a manner which most Northerners could not construe as threatening or violent; they dramatized the brutality of a system which would not give basic human respect to black Americans; they demanded incredible discipline, sacrifice, and mutual confidence from the demonstrators, thereby forging a human bond indispensable to a movement; and they provided an ideal vehicle for broadcasting to the nation the message of the movement and its quest for support. Perhaps most important, the sit-ins embodied in action the new vision of community that was the movement's essence—people coming together out of mutual conviction to express their belief in themselves, their rejection of an older way of doing things, and their affirmation of a fundamentally different perception of how life could be.[19]

For women activists the consciousness-raising session served a similar purpose. Begun in the civil rights and student movements as a means for women to express to each other their common sense of grievance, the consciousness-raising group quickly became the principal means for giving women a sense of solidarity and a vehicle for probing their common experience of sex discrimination. The result was the development in a supportive atmosphere of a profound feeling of grievance and commitment to change. Whether in a radical commune, a university community, or a corporation where women simply chose to get together to talk (never using the words consciousness-raising), the women's group helped to address the major problem faced by women in the past —the absence of an institution for expressing both solidarity and concern. As Gerda Lerner has observed, within a woman's group "reticence and the inability to speak out soon vanish in a supportive atmosphere. Members freely share their experiences and thoughts with one another, learn to reveal themselves, and develop feelings of solidarity and love for women . . . the effect of the group is to free the energy of its members and channel them into action." For women throughout the country who became active in one form or another of the women's movement, the discussion group served as the basic forum for developing a sense of strength, solidarity, and commitment. It thereby provided the "social space" for women to grow into a new perception of themselves, and move on to activities devoted to eliminating sex discrimination.[20]

Perhaps the most compelling parallel, however, is the extent to which activism brought growing numbers of blacks and women to reject the norms of the dominant culture and embark on a course of self-definition and determination. Throughout American history, both black and female protestors have been torn between strategies of identifying with the dominant values of the culture or rejecting them. For the most part, dissidents from both groups have taken the opportunities available to white males as the standard of what should be open to everyone. Thus black integrationists announced as their goal full participation in all segments of the society, including joint access to and involvement in the major institutions of white America. Similarly, women protestors have demanded that they be treated in the same way as men in seeking jobs and political influence. There have always been members of both groups, of course, who advocated either separatism or the development of a distinctive set of values, but overall, emulation of the dominant culture has been a primary theme of protest groups.

One of the consequences of this strategy, however, has been a tendency to accept the opposition's ground rules and premises. Those wishing access to the "system" frequently have absorbed the values, customs, and language of those in power. Hence, upwardly mobile blacks have tried to "make it" on the white man's terms, dressing and acting by white middle-class standards and even adopting similar political and social views. Aspiring career women, in turn, frequently have accepted general cultural views of female character traits as a means of solidifying their own acceptance, rather than endanger their status by demanding a revision of cultural norms. Thus, for example, Frances Perkins, the first woman Cabinet member and Secretary of Labor under Franklin Roosevelt, often endorsed the notion that woman's "place" was in the home and that married women in particular should not abandon their responsibilities there for the sake of making money.[21]

As both black protest and women's liberation developed during the 1960's, a growing number of more militant activists started to question this strategy of accepting the dominant culture's standards. Despite the major changes accomplished through remedial legislation, many of the less obvious means of social control, such as the socialization process and psychological manipulation, remained intact. Statutes which outlawed economic discrimination or attempted to ensure equal opportunity could not eradicate the subtle cultural and social pressures to conform to one's "place." In addition, as Cynthia Fuchs Epstein has shown in her study of prospective career women, one of the most effective forms of sex discrimination has been to exclude women from the interpersonal and informal networks where the "bright young men" are chosen. Thus, some of the more radical proponents of change in both movements emphasized the need to reassess the strategy of reform legislation and working within the values of the existing system. They directed their energies, instead, toward breaking the bonds of socialization and shifting the cultural ground rules.[22]

One manifestation of this development was the revival in both groups of a demand for a study of their respective pasts. Richard Wright had observed in *Black Boy* that "nothing about the problems of Negroes was ever taught in the classrooms at school; and whenever I would raise those questions with the boys, they would either remain silent or turn the subject into a joke. They were vocal about the petty individual wrongs they suffered, but they possessed no desire for a knowledge of the picture as a whole." In the 1960's the creation of women's studies and black studies programs seemed part of a common effort to recover an independent heritage within which to define one's self and develop a basis for relating to the dominant culture. Since women and blacks in the past had been alienated from their own history (and, some thought, intentionally taught to devalue themselves), they needed to recover a positive sense of self as a means of combating the control of the dominant cultural system. Though many criticized the academic justification and merits of such programs, activists in both movements saw them as central to declaring independence from those in the society who in the past had defined black and female history *for* those groups.

The same theme was manifested in the attention activists of both groups paid to common language usage. Words like "chick" or "girl" were only the most obvious examples of language that communicated the powerful social message that women were to be dealt with as sex objects and not quite adult people. The daily vocabulary of the society was full of even more subtle references, including the use of Mrs. and Miss as a means of defining women by their relationship to men—hence, not allowing women to be defined on their own terms. Black activists insisted on a similar control over the words used to describe them. The term "Negro," though still used by many, came to be viewed as a white label rather than a term growing out of the black community itself. Attention to Africanisms grew stronger as black Americans sought to re-establish links with their past. New styles of dress, more frequent usage of African words (*uhuru,* for example, as a synonym for freedom), and reliance on external signs of cultural distinctiveness such as an "Afro" hair style or African jewelry became badges of a new independence from the dominant white culture. Women activists, with their conscious rejection of the ornaments of consumer costuming such as makeup, girdles, and dresses, engaged in the same kind of rebellion against how others had defined them.

Not surprisingly, dissidents from both groups insisted also on changing the etiquettes of race and sex. Supporters of women's liberation refused to be treated as delicate or helpless creatures who needed doors opened for them or special assistance to sit down at a table. Such treatment, they reasoned, was only the benevolent side of a process, the malevolent side of which involved exclusion from important decisions, the best jobs, and equal rights of sex and self-assertion. Militant blacks, in turn, pointed out the paternalism of whites who wished to do "for" them those things that, by implication, they could not do themselves. Blacks who accepted white sponsorship for membership in private clubs were denounced by militants as "Toms" whose support of tokenism was aiding the enemy. Instead, reliance on members of one's own group for intellectual, emotional, and social support became the norm for the more angry members of both the women's movement and the black movement.

Perhaps the most radical manifestation of the new trend was the insistence of some members of both groups on total separatism. The evolution of black nationalism as a political strategy and a cultural way of life had as one of its purposes the announcement to white America that blacks would set their own standards, determine their own values, and establish their own institutions, no longer permitting whites to dictate the rules of the game. Some radical women set out to accomplish the same goal. Emphasizing the need of women to be "woman-identified" and not to take any portion of their self-image from dependence on men, they worked to build a network of institutions from printing presses to credit unions to feminist communes and health clinics as a means of declaring independence from the institutions and mores of the dominant culture.

Whatever the efficacy or validity of these individual efforts at cultural revolt, there seemed to be an underlying parallel implicit in the activities of both women and black protestors. Some members of both groups believed that the possibilities for further change depended at least in part on *who* defined the problems, *how* the problems were perceived, and what range of options was considered. According to this reasoning, as long as the rules were set by those who held power, there could only be as much substantive improvement as was consistent with the perpetuation of the society as it existed. Clearly, most Wall Street brokers would define the problem of poverty differently than would a welfare mother from Harlem. Reflecting this belief, both black and female activists asserted the need to reject the traditional view of their problems offered by the dominant society. Unless people defined themselves and determined their own agenda, they argued, those in power would set the ground rules and thus control the outcome of the game. In this sense, more militant female and black activists argued that separatism was a basic step toward making it possible for each group to interact with the dominant culture on its own terms. Although theoretically a sound strategy, as evidenced by the success of ethnic groups with strong separate institutions, this approach also presumed a willingness to use one's independent base as a departure point for coalition and interaction with groups inside of the dominant culture—an element of the strategy largely missing in the discussions of the late 60's and the 70's.

The ultimate irony of the separatist parallel, of course, was that precisely because dissident women and blacks insisted on cultural autonomy and self-determination, the possibilities for working together within a unified alliance became less and less. As Catharine Stimpson observed, "blacks must liberate themselves from whites, including white women; women must liberate themselves from men, including black men. Everyone's liberation must be self-won." If such a conclusion made less than likely a coalition of diverse groups, it also illustrated how closely black and women activists shared certain processes of development as they approached the question of how to bring about change in their own lives.[23]

There remains, finally, an intriguing, substantive connection in the sex/race analogy—the complicated interrrelationship of white and black women activists in the cause of both black and female liberation. Despite significant differences, a pattern of some cooperation between white women and black women has historically existed on issues of human rights. The diaries of at least some white Southern women in the ante-bellum period, Anne Firor Scott has pointed out, show sensitivity to the plight of the slave, and recognition of the fact that both women and slaves were powerless to change their condition. Other women, both North and South, fueled the abolitionist crusade with their energies and writing. Throughout the late 19th and early 20th century, it was again women among the white population who were most likely to show concern about racial oppression. Through the YWCA, Methodist Women's Missionary Societies, the Committee on Inter-Racial Cooperation, and the Association of Southern women for the Prevention of Lynching, some white women expressed a commitment to modify the racial status quo. In almost any community during the 20th century, especially in the South, women were more likely than men to be in the forefront of any effort toward inter-racial cooperation.[24]

The more dramatic side of the story, however, is the pivotal, initiating role played by black women in spurring white women to action. Throughout the reform movements of the 20th century involving race, it has most often been the courage, strength, and boldness of black women to which white women have responded. As Jacquelyn Dowd Hall has demonstrated strikingly in her work on the anti-lynching movement, black women initially defined the problem, set out to act on it, and in one way or another compelled a white response. In the late 19th century Ida B. Wells was most prominently associated with the antilynching drive. In the 1920's it was Lugenia Burns Hope and a group of Atlanta black women who carried the fight for integration to the YWCA national board, and continually challenged white women to show their commitment to working together for inter-racial cooperation. In 1922 the NAACP sponsored an organization of black women crusaders against lynching—an organization which enrolled 900 members in three months, despite the refusal of white women's groups to enlist in the campaign. Finally, in the early 1920's a group of black women led by Charlotte Hawkins Brown and Margaret Washington addressed a meeting of white church-women in Memphis, passionately urging a program of cooperative effort to secure racial justice in the areas of voting, education, and employment. Their eloquent presentation, and the emotional fervor it generated, led to the formation of the Women's Committee of the Commission on Inter-Racial Cooperation, the immediate forerunner of the anti-lynching campaign.[25]

Perhaps the most significant interaction, though, came in the civil rights movement of the 1960's. In a story brilliantly told by Sara Evans, black women again played a crucial role in sparking feminist consciousness among white women, particularly in SNCC. As white women from the South joined the movement, they were continually inspired by examples of black women who, in Sara Evans' words, "shattered cultural images of appropriate female behavior." Not only did black women students from colleges like Spelman and Bennett take to the streets to demand their freedom in communities such as Atlanta and Greensboro; their older counterparts actually held the movement together. In every Southern town, SNCC leader Charles Sherrod said, there were "Mamas" who provided the organizational base for action against the white power structure, coordinating food, shelter, transportation, jail visits, and other life-support activities. The result of all this, as one white Southern woman observed, was that "for the first time I had role models I could respect."

It was also black women in SNCC who were the first to comment and then act upon the system of male dominance which characterized the civil rights movement as well as the rest of society. In 1964 black women in the SNCC office took part in a half humorous, half serious sit-in to protest the fact that women were given sex-typed jobs such as always doing the clerical work. Later, there occurred a more serious dispute over who would take notes at a staff meeting, the argument resolved this time by use of a tape recorder.

Meanwhile, in a much more complicated way the issue of sexual relationships between people within the movement—especially black men and white women—eroded much of the sense of community which had previously existed among women across race lines. As more and more white women from the North entered the movement, a pattern of increased sexual interaction developed. In at least some cases, sleeping with a black man was viewed by white women as evidence of commitment to integration and the movement. On the other side, sleeping with white women became for some black men a symbolic political action as well as a physical and emotional one, demonstrating rebellion against white control by flouting the ultimate taboo. Understandably, the issue quickly became divisive, and black women in particular saw the emerging pattern as a threat.[26]

In this context of growing internal conflict, Ruby Doris Smith Robinson, a powerful black woman within SNCC, delivered a paper to a SNCC staff conference decrying the treatment of women in SNCC. A veteran of the earlier protest against sex discrimination in the SNCC office, she angrily attacked both the failure of black men to do justice toward black women, and the extreme insensitivity of Northern white women. The Robinson paper acted as a catalyst for Mary King and Casey Hayden,* two Southern white women who had long been active in SNCC. Hayden and King had taken part in earlier discussions with Robinson on the subject

* Her real name was Sondra Cason, but she became known as Casey Hayden.

but had backed away from a public statement. Now, stimulated by the Robinson presentation and deeply upset by a breakdown of "beloved community" in the movement, they composed their own statement, focusing on the common oppression shared by black and white women on the basis of sex. The King/Hayden manifesto later would be viewed as one of the opening statements of the women's liberation movement.[27]

In retrospect, two themes developed by Sara Evans seem especially worthy of comment. First, the protest carried out by the black women of SNCC reflected at the very least a strong incipient sense of feminism. Whether or not participants in the protests had developed a fully articulated theory of women's rights was immaterial. The substance of feminism was present, visible for others to see. Second, it seems plausible, if not likely, that the theory of women's oppression presented by Mary King and Casey Hayden developed initially out of a desire to present a basis for reconciliation between white women and black women in the movement. As Southern white women who had been through a great deal with black women in the movement prior to the arrival of the Northern students, they felt a sense of rejection and hurt over the divisions which the Northern intervention had brought. Out of that hurt, and from a growing but still uncrystallized sense of grievance as women, there emerged the manifesto of shared oppression which initially was to serve as a foundation for reconciliation within the movement, and later became a rallying cry for action outside the movement.

Perhaps appropriately the end of the story demonstrates the accuracy of Catharine Stimpson's perception that "everyone's liberation must be self-won." Although the declaration of sisterhood composed by Hayden and King was born of a desire to reconcile white women with black women, it came at precisely the moment that tensions within SNCC over race were reinforcing the move toward Black Power and greater emphasis on separatism. Thus the call for a separate women's consciousness coincided with the drive toward a separate black consciousness, signifying a lowering, for the moment at least, of the possibility for inter-racial cooperation.

Ironically, even the substantive ties between the women's movement and the black movement point more to a similarity of process than an identity of condition. For all that they shared together, the black and white women of SNCC had distinctive perspectives and priorities which eventually sent them on separate paths. Yet it was also fitting that the parallel movement which they made toward separate consciousness grew out of a momentary intersecting of experiences, highlighting the intricate and sometimes inextricable connection of race and sex as issues in American society. As much as any other example, in fact, the story of SNCC women demonstrates the value of exploring the questions of sex and race in relation to each other.

In the end, of course, the case for the analogy rests on the total picture, and the comparable processes of social control and social change which have evolved around the two issues. Both have been central to the structuring of the entire society, each functioning in its own way as a fundamental reference point for dividing power and responsibility. Each, in turn, has generated forms of social control designed to perpetuate those patterns of power and responsibility. Finally, the changes which occurred in the areas of sex and race after 1940 have also reflected a similar pattern, involving progression through parallel stages toward the development of collective action. In both cases it took an event of the magnitude of World War II to break the existing cycle of social control. Growing tension between norms and reality, in turn, provided fuel for protest. And after a crucial event which served as a catalyst, activists from both groups developed an innovative organizing tactic which in each case symbolized collective protest and served as an embodiment of group aims and purposes. The increasing conviction among more militant members of both groups that they needed to define their own identity and reject the dominant culture's view of their "problem" simply represented the last common stage in the process of change.

Whether the involvement of sex and race in comparable processes of change would lead to similar results could not be foretold. In some respects the question shifted emphasis back to substantive conditions rather than analogous processes. Whatever the case, the degree to which the issues of sex and race have entailed similar forms of control and comparable prerequisites for change appears to constitute that "resemblance" of attributes and circumstances necessary to justify making the analogy; and the analogy in turn illuminates significantly the basic workings of American society.

V.

Feminism
in the 1970's:
An Historical Perspective

The resurgence of feminism in the 1960's represented the third incarnation of a dynamic women's rights movement in American history. The first, as we have seen, grew out of the abolitionist struggle of the 1830's and featured the legendary leadership of people like Elizabeth Cady Stanton and Susan B. Anthony. The second developed out of the social reform ethos of the early 1900's, and though the lineal descendant of the first movement, exhibited a style of leadership and a tactical approach significantly different from its antecedent. Cresting with the battle over the suffrage amendment, it succumbed to factionalism and public indifference in the 1920's and 1930's. The contemporary movement, like its predecessors, has grown out of a period of generalized social ferment, both drawing upon and reflecting a widespread sensitivity toward discrimination and injustice. The contemporary drive for women's liberation, however, differs from its forerunners in at least three ways: it is grounded in and moving in the same direction as underlying social trends at work in the society; it has developed an organizational base that is diverse and decentralized; and it is pursuing a wide range of social objectives that strike at many of the root causes of sex inequality. Although some of these distinctive characteristics are a source of weakness as well as strength, no previous feminist movement has attempted so much, and none has been better situated to make progress toward the goal of equality.

Probably the chief advantage of contemporary feminism lies in the extent to which its goals and programs have meshed with, or addressed directly, prevailing trends in the society. In the past, the demands of women's rights organizations had often been far removed from the experience and immediate concerns of most women in the population. Although the Seneca Falls Declaration of Sentiments and Resolutions was bold in its vision, it bore little relationship to the world most women found themselves in—a world that was non-urban, populated by large families, and increasingly suffused with the precepts of Victorian morality. The notions of equal access to careers, or being able to preach from the pulpit, appealed to only a select group of women. Indeed, feminist objectives were so far outside the realm of most people's experience that females and males alike tended to dismiss early women's rights advocates as a lunatic fringe.

In a slightly different way, the suffrage movement of the 20th century also displayed misunderstanding of, and lack of contact with, some of the basic realities of the day. In their quest for one of the most fundamental rights of citizenship—the vote—the suffragists overestimated the extent to which a breakthrough in one area would lead to liberation in others as well. By expecting all women to vote together for the same candidates and programs on the basis of loyalty to their sex, the suffragists profoundly misread the degree to which ethnic, class, and family allegiances undermined the prospect of sex-based political behavior. Similarly, in thinking that winning the vote would encourage women to carry the fight for equality into the economic arena as well, the suffragists underestimated significantly the power of traditional forces of socialization. In both cases the fundamental error was to exaggerate the ability of a political reform to transform an entire structure of roles and activities based on gender.[1]

The one area where "emancipation" did take hold—that of sex—also illustrated the extent to which the suffragists were out of touch with some of the trends in society. Throughout the first three decades of the 20th century, a sexual revolution was in progress. For women born after 1900, rates of premarital and extra-marital intercourse were approximately double those of women born before 1900. A new awareness of contraceptive devices and an increased recognition of female sexuality signified an important expansion of sexual freedom for middle-class women of the flapper era. Yet many feminists were repelled by the "revolution in manners and morals." To most women's rights advocates, the flapper seemed frivolous and irresponsible. At a time when there were political battles to be fought and careers to be opened up, concern with the libido and sexual freedom appeared counter-productive. Sex was meant for procreation, Charlotte Perkins Gilman remarked, and her views seemed to reflect the generalized dismay of suffrage leaders about the new morality. Improving the status of women in government and the economy required discipline, dedication, and sacrifice—attributes seemingly inconsistent with the concerns dominating the lives of younger women.[2]

In the end, of course, it was the social environment rather than the shortcomings of women activists which prevented the realization of feminist hopes. As long as the day-to-day structure of most women's lives reinforced the existing distribution of sex roles, there was little possibility of developing a feminist constituency committed to far-reaching change. Women in large numbers might support the effort to win the suffrage, but there was no frame of reference in experience, and little support in the culture, for seeking the kind of full-scale equality that would revolutionize the social structure. Although the suffragists participated in the general "progressive" tendency to equate limited reforms with basic change, the real problem was a social milieu which proved inhospitable to more far-reaching change.

In this context, the feminism of the 1960's and 1970's differed from previous women's movements precisely because it grew out of and built upon prevailing social trends. For the first time ideological protest and underlying social and economic changes appeared to be moving in a similar direction. As we have seen already, female work patterns were virtually transformed in the years after 1940. Prior to World War II, female employment was limited primarily to young, single women or poor, married women. Few middle-class wives held jobs. By 1975, in contrast, the two-income family had become the norm; 49 per cent of all wives worked; and the median income of families where wives were employed was nearly $17,000. Although the employment changes did not signify progress toward equality, they ensured that social norms about woman's "place" no longer had a base in reality.*

As a result, feminist programs spoke more directly than ever before to the daily experience of millions of women. Female workers might not consider themselves feminists; indeed, they might shun any kind of association with the abstract cause of women's rights. But the same workers knew that they did not receive equal pay with men and that most of the higher paying jobs carried a "male only" tag. Similarly, the large number of women workers who had school-age and pre-school children understood the problems caused by inadequate day-care and after-school facilities. Discontented homemakers, who yearned for a more diverse life but saw all the barriers in the way, had a comparable sense of recognition. Thus there developed a common ground on which feminist activists and their potential constituency could stand, and that common ground provided the starting point from which some women moved toward greater collective consciousness of a sense of grievance.[3]

A second social trend which coincided with the revival of feminism was the decline in the birth rate during the 60's and 70's. After World War II a "baby boom" swept the country, peaking in 1957 with a birth rate of 27.2 children per thousand people. There then ensued a prolonged downturn, which in 1967 resulted in a birth rate of 17.9, the lowest since the Great Depression. At the time demographers disagreed about the reasons for the decline, some citing the development of oral contraceptives, others economic and social instability. But all agreed there would be a new baby boom in the early 1970's when the children born twenty years earlier began to reproduce. Instead of rising, though, the birth rate continued to plummet, reaching an all-time

* In fact, income differentials between men and women increased over time, and most women were employed in low-paying positions which offered no chance for advancement.

low by the mid-70's and achieving the reproduction level required—over time—for Zero Population Growth.

Although many forces contributed to the continuing decline, the interaction of female employment with changing attitudes toward women's roles appears to have been decisive. Throughout the 1960's, women married later, delayed the birth of their first child, and bore their last child at an earlier age. Whether as cause or effect, this trend coincided with many women finding occupations and interests away from the home. The rewards of having a job, as well as the desire for extra money to meet rising living standards, tended to emphasize the advantages of a small family. These values, in turn, were reinforced in the late 60's by the ideology of feminism and the population control movement. Two Gallup polls in 1967 and 1971 highlighted the shift in values. The earlier survey showed that 34 per cent of women in the prime childbearing years anticipated having four or more children. By 1971, in contrast, the figure had dropped to 15 per cent. Two years later 70 per cent of the nation's 18- to 24-year-old women indicated that they expected to have no more than two children. Thus feminist emphasis on personal fulfillment and freedom from immersion in traditional sex roles operated in tandem with long-range social developments which made such goals more objectively feasible.[4]

Finally, changing attitudes and behavior in the realm of human sexuality meshed closely with feminist values concerning personal and bodily liberation. Although suffrage leaders in the early 20th century had exhibited little understanding or tolerance of the sexual revolution, supporters of women's liberation emphasized as one of their strongest themes the importance of women knowing their own bodies and having the freedom to use them as they saw fit. One manifestation of this emphasis was the publication by a woman's health collective of *Our Bodies Our Selves,* a handbook which urged women to understand and appreciate their bodies. (The book had sold 850,000 copies from 1971 through 1976.) Still another manifestation was a generally supportive attitude toward "liberated" personal life-styles, including lesbianism, communal living, and sexual relationships outside of marriage.

Significantly, such attitudes reinforced many of the social trends already developing in the culture, particularly among the young. In the eyes of many observers, a second sexual revolution occurred starting in the mid-60's. One study of women students at a large urban university showed a significant increase after 1965 in the number of women having intercourse while in a "dating" or "going steady" relationship; at the same time guilt feelings about sex sharply declined. Another nation-wide sample of freshmen college women in 1975 disclosed that one-third endorsed casual sex based on a short acquaintance, and over 40 per cent believed a couple should live together before getting married. Most indicative of changing mores, perhaps, was a survey of eight colleges in 1973 which showed not only that 76 per cent of women had engaged in intercourse by their junior year (the male figure was 75 per cent), but that women were appreciably more active sexually than men. Daniel Yankelovich's public opinion polls of college and non-college young people in the 60's and 70's appeared to confirm the major departure in sexual behavior and attitudes. Only a minority of women disapproved morally of pre-marital sex, homosexual relations between consenting adults, or having an abortion. Although women's liberation advocates warned that women could be victimized anew as sex objects under the guise of sexual freedom (just as they had been under a system of more repressive mores), the fact remained that the movement's support for abortion, homosexual rights, and free bodily expression placed it more in harmony with emerging cultural attitudes toward sexuality than in opposition.[5]

In each of these areas, it seemed clear that the women's liberation movement was both drawing upon and reinforcing important changes taking place in the society. Shifts in employment patterns, demography, and sexual mores may have had a momentum of their own, but feminism introduced a powerful ingredient of ideology and activism that sought to transform these impersonal social trends and create new values and attitudes toward sex roles. In that sense, for the first time a dynamic relationship existed between "objective" social changes and feminist efforts to shape those changes in a particular direction. In contrast with each of the previous woman's movements, the women's liberation drive of the 1960's and 1970's operated in a context where the social preconditions for ideological change were present. No longer was feminism irrelevant to most people's daily lives. Instead, its message spoke to many of the realities of the contemporary society. As a result, the possibility of an audience being able to respond was greater than ever before.

The second major distinctive quality of the new feminism is that as a result of a broader social base, the organization and structure of the movement differ significantly from that of the past. When women's rights advocates were on the margin of society and alienated from the world of most women, the organizational basis of the movement was narrow. Supporters of feminism, for the most part, came from the same social class and economic background. To maximize impact, the organizations they formed were national in scope. The women's liberation movement of the 60's and 70's, in contrast, almost defied categorization. Although feminist groups such as NOW and the Women's Equity Action League (WEAL) operated out of national offices in a style similar to that of other reform groups, the grass roots supporters of the movement fit less easily into an organizational niche. Some observers described women's liberation as a "guerilla movement," its headquarters located in every kitchen or bedroom where women developed a more critical and independent sense of self. Whether or not the description was fully accurate, the new feminism appeared both diverse and decentralized, its strength more likely to be found in local communities than in national hierarchies. Since the movement had emerged in response to social conditions affecting a large number of women, it tended to reflect the different backgrounds of its supporters and the special concerns which were of greatest interest to them.

The distinction between the various feminist movements was reflected in their different constituencies. Through most of the 19th century, feminism drew its support primarily from a scattering of upper- and upper-middle-class women

who were angered at the growing tendency to deny women
the opportunity to use their abilities on the same basis as
men. Although occasional working-class women or black
heroines like Sojourner Truth joined the movement, feminism
was generally identified with radical, alienated members of
the cultural elite. Toward the beginning of the 20th century, the movement softened its rhetoric and broadened its
base, becoming part of the larger effort of Progressive reform.
But it remained overwhelmingly native white and middle
class. Suffrage organizations shared the anti-black and anti-
immigrant prejudices of their age, passing resolutions that
disparaged both groups. Despite achieving a remarkable
amount of support from club women and church women, the
suffragists, like the Progressives generally, represented a homogeneous middle-class constituency.

With some justification, the same charge of being narrow,
elitist, and white middle class has also been leveled at the
women's liberation movement. In the late 60's feminism was
generally associated with "liberal" university towns, student
enclaves, the affluent suburbs, or the cosmopolitan urban
centers of the East and West Coasts. Many supporters of the
movement did come from the best universities and from well-
off families, even if in the latter case, they had rejected some
of the paraphernalia of affluence. (In a survey of its readers,
Ms. magazine found that 84 per cent had been to college, and
that 71 per cent worked, mostly in higher level jobs.) Others
supposedly were disaffected suburban wives and mothers,
bored by bridge parties and chauffering children to dance lessons. From the point of view of some critics, such women
were indulging a fantasy desire to join the world of social
protest, and in the absence of exposure to the real injustices
of hunger, poverty, and racial violence had "invented" the
superficial issue of sex discrimination.

Still, the charge of elitism appeared less applicable to the
women's movement of the 60's and 70's than to prior manifestations of feminism. Most supporters of the movement
identified with the political left and were highly conscious of
the issues of class and race, seeking wherever possible to find
ways of transcending those barriers. Rather than criticize or

remain aloof from other dissident groups, women libera-
tionists supported organizations like the United Farm Workers and aligned themselves with other groups seeking social
change. (The early women's rights movement had done the
same, of course, but the concern with racism faded by the
late 19th century.) Many of the substantive demands of the
movement, in turn, promised to help the poor as well as
the rich and middle class. Most well-off women could afford
to send their children to nursery school or hire service help.
It was working-class women who would benefit most from
universal day-care, equal pay, an end to job discrimination,
and the availability of inexpensive abortions and birth control
assistance.

In addition, there was some evidence to contradict the
popular image of the women's movement as a white middle-
class preserve. Despite major differences in priority and perspective between black and white women, a National Black
Feminist Organization formed in 1973 both to assert the distinctive interests of black women in the struggle for wom-
en's rights and to provide a base for cooperative action on
those issues which affected women across racial lines. By
1974 the NBFO had a membership of 2,000 women in ten
chapters.* Similarly, working-class women affirmed some
identification with the concerns of the women's movement
through the creation of the Coalition of Labor Union Women
(CLUW). When the new organization met in Chicago in
1973 over 3000 women from a wide range of unions united
on a platform with clear feminist overtones. Although most
of the issues were economic, the dominant theme was that
women, as women, shared a reason to organize and fight for
their collective interest. Earlier in the 20th century the Wom-
en's Trade Union League (WTUL) sought to achieve objectives which sounded similar but, despite some attention to
unionizing activities, the WTUL was primarily a Progressive,

---

* In addition it should be noted that black women have been stronger
supporters of the idea of women's liberation than white women. A 1972
Louis Harris poll for Virginia Slims showed blacks outscoring whites 62 to
45 per cent in support of efforts to change women's status, and 67 to 35
per cent on sympathy with women's liberation groups.

middle-class organization devoted to persuading middle-class citizens to support social welfare legislation. CLUW, in contrast, excluded non-union members and seemed committed to a working-class perspective tied to relevant feminist issues. Significantly, a poll by Social Research Inc. showed substantial suport for feminist goals (though not feminist tactics) among working-class women. Thus, even if most avowed feminists were white and middle class in origin, the nature of the movement's involvement with women of diverse social and economic backgrounds suggested a more varied constituency than had existed in the past.[6]

Perhaps more important, the new social base of feminism produced a thoroughly decentralized structure. When feminism had a narrower constituency, activity tended to focus on a national or state level. Hoping to maximize their influence, women reformers joined together in committees dedicated to securing specific goals such as the suffrage, or a minimum wage bill for women. A few devoted activists would work out of a regional or national headquarters, and in the name of all women, seek to persuade legislators or public opinion leaders of the virtue of their cause. Even when the popular base of the movement broadened in the early 20th century, the structure remained hierarchical, with coordination starting from state and national levels and working down to local branches. Indeed, through most of the 19th and 20th centuries, feminist groups were characterized by a vertical structure in which activity centered in coordinating committees at the top.

The women's liberation movement of the 60's and 70's, in contrast, was almost without any overarching structure. Despite the existence of groups like the National Organization of Women (NOW), the movement functioned primarily through small, informal groups on a local level. Its energy came from the bottom, not the top, and from the immediate ongoing concern of women with the quality of their own lives. Events or issues which were national in scope (such as the Equal Rights Amendment, or the march for equality on the 50th anniversary of the suffrage victory) were certainly not ignored, but the day-to-day direction of the movement grew out of local conditions which were central to the lives of the women most involved. Thus, as long as people in the immediate environment shared a common sense of grievance and a common desire for change, the movement was largely self-sustaining. It did not depend on national leadership. Indeed, many feminists believed deeply that "leaders" were unnecessary, that women could make decisions collectively, and that concepts of hierarchy and command were products of a male culture, hence to be avoided. In this context, the movement was decentralized for two reasons: it was rooted in local communities where women came together to deal with issues in their own lives; and it represented an ideology that viewed large organizations and leadership structures as part of the problem rather than the solution.*

Not surprisingly, the absence of conventional leadership structures proved a source of considerable controversy. Some observers criticized the movement for its lack of direction and focus, implying that a disciplined national organization could mobilize a concerted following and secure more immediate results. Women's liberation theorist Jo Freeman warned about a potential "tyranny of structurelessness," arguing that the deliberate rejection of structure by feminists could create situations where a few women with staying power would dominate the movement because of the absence of regularized procedures to guarantee fairness and order. The latter criticism, in particular, spoke to a perennial problem. The entire Judeo-Christian tradition was premised on the imperfection of human nature, and the tendency of people, in the absence of external restraints, to seek their own ends. Reliance on collective good will, without resort to institutionalized checks and balances, tested severely people's ability to withstand the temptation to take advantage of others and impose their own

* Despite decentralization, a substantial network of interpersonal and intra-movement communication created a sense of participation in a national movement. Whether through collective books such as *The New Woman's Survival Catalogue,* feminist newsletters which criss-crossed the country, *Ms.* magazine, or cultural vehicles such as women's liberation rock bands, activists maintained some contact which reinforced local energies and counteracted isolation.

will. Indeed, among some student radical groups, outlasting the opposition during interminable meetings provided a basic technique for controlling—and abusing—the process of participatory democracy.[7]

In addition, the absence of structure helped to narrow the movement's class base, and limit its political effectiveness. Informal meetings worked well when people were skillful with words, confident about handling social tension, and at ease with complex and open-ended relationships. But not everyone fit such a category. Working-class people in particular favored meetings of limited duration with a specific agenda and a structured format. Moreover, the emphasis of movement supporters on intra-group compatibility unintentionally reinforced a tendency toward middle-class homogeneity. Also, an absence of structure made effective political action less likely. Not only was there no identifiable hierarchy to speak for the movement in developing coalitions or negotiating issues; the emphasis on "personal" issues sometimes diverted attention from public policy.[8]

On balance, though, it seemed that decentralization and the lack of structure were central to the movement's strength ae well as its distinctiveness. An ideal social movement might combine the discipline of a national organization with the energy of local grass roots efforts, yet such a combination appeared inconsistent—even contradictory—to the internal dynamics of the women's liberation movement. The vitality of the movement lay precisely in the proliferation of local organizations, each growing out of a particular concern or experience of different groups of women. Because such organizations reflected the immediate priorities of the women who created them, they commanded substantial loyalty and energy. It seemed at least possible, if not likely, that such an investment of local energy and initiative would be difficult to sustain in a hierarchical organization with established policies and strict procedures.

Finally, the pattern of decentralization ensured that the women's liberation movement would not rise or fall on the basis of one organization's activities or decisions. When all attention was riveted on a single national group as the embodiment of a cause, there was always the danger of defeat through internal divisions or the independent action of third parties. Thus some movements have been judged dead or alive on the basis of a single vote in Congress, or a series of public relations maneuvers. A social movement rooted in diverse local situations, however, and organized around a variety of issues, was less vulnerable to symbolic defeats. Thus, just as the movement's relevance to social trends helped to reinforce its ideological vitality, its decentralized structure accentuated its organizational strong point—grass roots support in the local community.

This, in turn, leads to the third distinguishing characteristic of the women's liberation movement, the variety and scope of its objectives. Through most of the 19th and 20th centuries, the women's movement tended to focus on a single issue, showing a tendency characteristic of nearly all American reform efforts. Although the Seneca Falls feminists sought far-reaching change in almost every area relevant to sex discrimination, their approach was too radical, and in a basically uncongenial political atmosphere it made sense to select one issue to effectively symbolize the movement. The problem was that the suffrage gradually became identified *in toto* with the larger issues. In a similar way, the National Women's Party (NWP) became obsessed with the belief that an Equal Rights Amendment (ERA) would prove to be a panacea. Beginning in 1923 the NWP devoted its entire energies to the fight for an ERA, eschewing identification with other questions such as birth control or maternal and infant health care. Clearly, the ERA was an important issue, and its incorporation into the Constitution would have provided a valuable lever for seeking change in woman's status wherever questions of law were involved. But in the process of seeking the ERA, the NWP, already a small elitist organization, alienated most working women (the ERA prior to 1941 would have brought invalidation of protective legislation for working women such as minimum-wage laws)*, spent an excessive amount of energy battling other women's organizations, and tended to ignore the extent to which the roots of sex inequality went beyond the reach of even the most powerful constitutional amendment.[9]

The supporters of women's liberation, on the other hand, appeared to recognize the pitfalls of thinking there was any single answer to inequality or sex role stereotyping. The result was a plethora of related but separate activities, giving each individual group maximum leeway to work on the specific aspect of inequality that concerned it most. Although ratification of the proposed Equal Rights Amendment to the Constitution, repeal of abortion laws, or women's political caucuses represented the most visible items on the feminist agenda, most activists understood that success in one venture only meant there would be a new problem to work on. In this sense, feminists seemed to have learned a great deal from the civil rights movement, where the achievement of some goals such as the Voting Rights Act simply disclosed the existence of additional layers of racism to be combated. Implicit in feminist activities was the perception that, as in the Chinese proverb, the problem of inequality was a box within a box within a box, with no single answer.

The spectrum of activities in one university community during the early 1970's illustrated the diversity of objectives pursued by different groups. One group of women came together to plan a course for public school teachers on eliminating sexism in the classroom. Another met weekly to edit and publish children's books which were free of invidious sex stereotypes. Still another group worked on a coalition of citizens concerned with day care. While a local woman's center sponsored a meeting for the purpose of starting a union of household workers, a NOW chapter worked to counter employment discrimination. Counseling on sexuality, birth control, and abortion occupied still others. Lesbian discussion

* In *U.S. v. Darby* the Supreme Court in 1941 for the first time upheld protective legislation for both sexes. Prior to that time it was assumed by most legal experts that an ERA would have compelled invalidation of protective legislation for women.

groups provided a forum for homosexual women to talk about the politics of sex, and a socialist feminist group addressed the junction of class and sex issues. Consciousness-raising groups for divorced or widowed women attempted to deal with the specific problems growing out of those situations. Although such diversity produced conflict over priorities as well as opportunities for cooperation, it illustrates the pluralistic approach which the women's movement of the 60's and 70's brought to the problem of sex inequality—an approach which maximized the possibility of local women becoming involved in an issue important to their own immediate lives.

In the end, therefore, each of the distinctive qualities of feminism in the 60's and 70's was inextricably connected to the next. Because feminist ideas directly addressed contemporary social realities, more people perceived the movement as revelant to their own circumstances. This, in turn, helped to produce involvement in local activities which seemed pertinent to the larger issue. The extent to which the movement grew out of and related back to the immediate experience of large numbers of women made unnecessary the centralized and hierarchical structures of the past, and the absence of such structures encouraged the development of multiple activities, each dealing with a particular aspect of sex inequality. In this sense, the women's liberation movement of the 60's and 70's was more similar to the Southern Farmer's Alliance of the 1880's or the civil rights movement of the 1960's than to earlier manifestations of feminism. It took its direction and vitality from the experience of people in local communities.

As in the history of all social movements, however, contemporary feminism faced serious obstacles. Some reflected internal tensions that emerged from the very diversity and decentralization which distinguished the movement from its predecessors. Others derived from outside sources and mirrored the opposition, tacit as well as organized, which the ideas of women's liberation engendered. Together, they highlighted both the dimensions of the challenge confronting the movement and the scope of its quest for change.

Perhaps the most profound obstacle was the extent to which the movement threatened the sense of identity millions of people had derived from the culture and from the primary transmitter of social values, the family. The words "masculine" and "feminine" were as emotionally powerful in the meanings they conveyed as any other terms, including "white" and "black." People were raised to identify as almost sacred the attributes attached to each phrase, and to view any deviation as a mark of shame. For a boy to be called a "fairy," for example, represented a crushing insult, to be avoided at all costs.

Those who were deeply committed to prevailing values, such as the author George Gilder, believed that such networks of attributes derived from a sexual constitution found in all civilized societies. Within that constitution, women controlled otherwise intemperate male drives by tying men to the family, giving them a bond of fatherhood to their progeny, building up the masculine role of provider, and rewarding the male sex drive through the act of genital intercourse. (Genital intercourse was important because it affirmed male dominance, was tied directly to procreation, and thus supported the maintenance of the sexual constitution.) Within this social system, all work found its "ultimate test in the quality of the home," and woman's role as housewife made hers the "central position in all civilized society." This position, in turn, derived from woman's part in procreation and the primary tie of mother and child. Thus, according to Gilder:

> The woman's sexual life and how she manages it is crucial to this process of male socialization. The males have no ties to women and children—or to long-term human community—so deep or tenacious as the mother's to her child. That is primary in society; all else is contingent and derivative. . . . The woman assumes charge of . . . the domestic values of the community. . . . all those matters that we consider of such importance that we do not ascribe a financial worth to them.

In this context, an assault on any components of the sexual constitution—childbirth, the male role as provider, or geni-

tal sex—threatened to destroy civilized society itself by unleash-
ing the previously harnessed anti-social drives of males.[10]

Whether or not others would agree with Gilder's description of the sources of civilized society, it seemed clear that
feminism was attacking the entire spectrum of traditional
male and female roles. Women's liberation advocates argued
that the culture had denied females their right to be human,
first, by insisting that they be "feminine" and, then, by
defining "feminine" in such a way that women were deprived
of the freedom to shape their own lives and choose their own
careers. The same culture, it was charged, had denied males
the right to be fully human by ruling out of bounds the idea
of fatherhood as a full-time vocation and defining as inappropriate for men the expression of vulnerability, gentleness, or
dependence. To correct these errors, feminists proposed to
dismantle or radically alter some of the fundamental institutions of the culture. Instead of the traditional marriage cere-
mony, feminists suggested a marital contract, specifying the
responsibilities of each partner and the prerequisites that had
to be maintained for the relationship to be continued. Women's liberation advocates argued that women and men
should be equally free to pursue careers, care for children,
initiate sex, and select social companions. Public day-care
services, they contended, should be available to assume part
of the responsibility previously borne solely by parents. And
individuals should be free —as individuals—to determine
their own life style, sexual preference, occupation, and personal values.

Not surprisingly, both the indictment and the proposed
solutions deeply offended people who had been raised to believe that existing norms of behavior were not only functional
but morally inviolable. If not everyone went as far as George
Gilder in seeing feminist views as leading to "sexual suicide,"
many nevertheless felt threatened. To women who had spent
a lifetime devoting themselves to the culturally sanctioned
roles of homemaker and helpmate, the feminist charge that
women had been enslaved frequently appeared as a direct attack on their own personal experience. Such women did not
believe that they had wasted their lives or had been duped by
malevolent husbands. Many enjoyed the nurturant and sup-

portive roles of wife and mother, believed that the family should operate with a sexual division of labor, and profoundly resented the suggestion that the life of a homemaker somehow symbolized failure. From their point of view, the women's liberation movement was often guilty of arrogance and contempt toward the majority of women, and some expressed that view by voting against local Equal Rights amendments in New Jersey and New York or by supporting the traditional values celebrated in the "Total Woman" movement.[11]

In a somewhat similar way, many men believed that the movement was conducting an insidious campaign to undermine their strength, deny their authority, and destroy their self-image. As they looked at feminist demands for equal sharing of household responsibilities, affirmative action in employment, and complete freedom over personal lives, it seemed that women activists were trying to take away their role as breadwinners and sabotage their position of leadership in the home. Instead of helping women, many men believed, feminists were intent on wrecking the family, turning wife against husband, and transforming men into dishwashers and baby-sitters. Nothing threatened men more than the belief that in movement groups women told each other intimate details of their respective experiences with men and hatched plans to subvert traditional marital relationships. From such a vantage point, women's liberation symbolized anarchic and amoral forces at work in the society, seeking to untie all the knots and loosen the bonds that gave life its security and stability.

Although such fears were exaggerated, concern about the challenge to traditional "masculine" and "feminine" roles ran deep in the society. The issues raised by feminism went to the root of people's personal as well as social identity. At best such questions had the potential of making people vulnerable and insecure. At worst, they produced bitter hostility. Moreover, there existed a generalized anxiety that the triumph of women's liberation might mean the destruction of human relationships as they had been known, with impersonal competition replacing the warmth associated with woman's traditional role, and a unisex sameness overcoming the rich distinctiveness of previous male-female relationships. Part nostalgia and part legitimate concern about depersonalization, the anxiety provided important kindling for those forces seeking to build a political backfire against women's liberation on such issues as opposition to abortion and the Equal Rights Amendment. Thus the greatest obstacle feminism faced was the commitment of millions of people to the institutions, values, and personal self-images which were associated with traditional sex roles. As conservatives mobilized the political potential implicit in that commitment, feminists found some of their objectives increasingly endangered.

The second major obstacle faced by the movement was that of internal dissension. Though the absence of a centralized structure and focus on a single issue proved to be assets in most respects, the resulting diversity of aims and priorities constituted a seedbed of ideological conflict. Intense factional disputes erupted over both goals and methods. Some feminists believed that only the total abolition of the nuclear family could bring freedom to women. Others accepted the family institution but sought to change its structure to make it more equitable. While some traced discrimination against women to an inherent and irrevocable male malevolence, others saw men as parallel victims of a warped socialization process. Similar divisions developed over the issue of style or political tactics. Should movement supporters denounce the status quo in uncompromising terms and demand immediate radical change? Or should they moderate their rhetoric, seek a common ground with their audience, and attempt to move one step at a time? Clearly, such questions had no easy answers, but they produced a continuing tension which on occasion resulted in internal disputes even more ferocious and embittered than conflicts with outside opponents.

A conference of socialist feminists held at Yellow Springs, Ohio, in the summer of 1975 highlighted some of the factional difficulties created by the diverse make-up of the movement. The more than 1500 participants at the conference were for the most part self-defined Marxists who sup-

posedly agreed that all oppression, whether based on class,
sex, race, or lesbianism, was inter-related, and that socialist
feminism, operating through an autonomous women's movement, provided the best strategy for revolution. With the
aim of recognizing variety and at the same time bringing
unity out of diversity, the conference planners scheduled
workshops on subjects ranging from women in prison to
women in farming and anarchist feminist experiments. Informal caucuses of Jewish women, older women, and mothers
also sprang up, each focusing on the particular concerns of
most significance to the particular group—older women, for
example, asking that attention be paid to the crises of employment, health, and family that frequently accompanied
middle age.

The major conflicts at the conference, however, erupted
over the radically different perceptions of the underlying
problem held by lesbian feminists, a third world caucus, and
an "anti-imperialist, Marxist-Leninist" caucus. The last-
named group insisted that class was the basic problem, that
women's organizations had to be subsumed within the revolutionary struggle of the proletariat, and that efforts to develop alternative life-styles to the family or an autonomous
women's movement were a *petit bourgeois* escape from the real
issue. Within this view, male supremacy and hierarchical
rule were simply a function of capitalism and once capitalism
was overthrown oppression of women and lesbians would
cease. Lesbian feminists, by contrast, argued that homosexuality represented more than a personal sexual preference and was a political act against the institutional source of
all women's oppression, heterosexuality. Within this perspective, male supremacy constituted the basic problem, and its
primary instrument of control was the heterosexual relationship.* Although capitalism was implicated in the problem, male supremacy also existed in socialist countries like

---

* The lesbian argument and that offered by George Gilder were interest-
ing variants of the same theme. In the one case genital intercourse was seen
as the basis of civilized society, in the other as the source of all female
oppression. Gilder, of course, saw it as a way of keeping men, not women,
in line.

Cuba, where homosexuals were oppressed and "macho" values remained largely intact. Thus only a direct attack on the source of male oppression could bring liberation for women; for that reason, all feminists had to identify, politically at least, with the lesbian struggle. Finally, the third world panel asserted the primacy of race and imperialism as fundamental questions. Pointing out the absence of many conference participants from third world backgrounds, the caucus warned of the dangers of generalizing from white middle-class experience, particularly involving the family, to third world cultures with different priorities and perspectives. A poor black woman, one speaker remarked, cared more about food and decent medical care than sophisticated feminist theorizing. By the end of the conference, therefore, instead of arriving at a "unified understanding of women's oppression," the women participants had been forced to grapple with most of the conflicts inherent in a movement which sought to speak for a group divided into multiple class, racial, and cultural constituencies. No event could have dramatized more the potential for factionalism.[12]

For the most part, supporters of the movement attempted to deal with the danger of dissension in two ways. First, there developed early in the movement a general policy of not excluding groups or points of view for reasons of political unorthodoxy or social unpopularity. The issue surfaced quickly on the question of endorsing the struggle of lesbians; despite deep concern among some that identification with homosexuality would harm the prospect of gaining legislative and political reform, most activists made common cause on the indivisibility of women's rights. In part this reflected the absence of a monolithic organization seeking to impose a party line, and in part an ideological conviction that disavowing one group of women for reasons of political expediency would lead to the death of the movement. A second approach—growing out of the first—was a belief that women could resolve conflict through understanding and conciliation. While men might go to war rather than admit the possibility of error, women, it was argued, could work through a problem to a collective solution. Thus observers at the Yellow Springs conference reported a desire on the part of the conflicting groups to deal with their differences "in the context of the whole," rather than to secede into separate bastions.

Not surprisingly, though, the depth of feeling sometimes divided the movement into warring camps. Gloria Steinem, identified in the public eye as a major feminist figure because of her writing and the attention paid her by the media, became a symbol of such divisions when she was accused by some "radical" feminists of having been a CIA agent for ten years. Because of her association with the "moderate" *Ms.* magazine and her reluctance to adopt an uncompromisingly radical stance on some issues, Steinem unwittingly became a scapegoat in the fight over who would control the movement. Conflicts between lesbians and non-lesbians also frequently reached the stage of no-holds-barred battle, and some feminists like Betty Friedan viewed the so-called "lavender menace" as more an enemy to the movement than male chauvinism. Even more established organizations like NOW split over the reform/radical issue, and when the 1975 NOW convention adopted as its slogan "out of the mainstream and into the revolution," some members withdrew in protest to start their own organization.[13]

Together with resistance to change within the dominant culture, then, the constant threat of internecine warfare plagued the movement's efforts to make inroads among its potential constituency. The questions at issue were neither trivial nor simple, and the distinction between compromise and surrender was not always clear. Yet there was a profound difference between viewing the contented homemaker as a deluded Sambo and reaching out to make contact with her on her own ground. Similarly, a tremendous chasm separated those who viewed men as congenitally oppressive and those who saw males as people in need of support as well as prodding in coming to grips with their attitudes. In the presence of such conflicts, the potential existed that the women's movement of the 1960's and 1970's would fall victim to the same polarization that had torn apart its predecessor in the

1920's, and that energies needed for positive action would be diverted into sectarian feuding.

Still, what remained impressive was the degree of change that appeared to be taking place notwithstanding the obstacles. Although most American women might disavow any overt association with the movement *per se* ("I'm no women's libber," "They're too radical for my taste"), the same women supported many of the substantive programs of the movement. Day-care centers, availability of abortion services, equal career opportunities, and greater sharing of household tasks all received substantial approval in public opinion surveys of women. As late as 1962 a Gallup poll showed that a majority of female respondents did not believe American women were discriminated against. Eight years later women divided down the middle on the question of whether they supported the movement to secure greater equality. By 1974 those responding to the same question endorsed the efforts toward more equality by two to one.[14]

The greatest impact of the movement appeared among the young and on college campuses. The Yankelovich survey of the early 70's showed a doubling in two years of the number of students viewing women as an oppressed group, with a large majority endorsing concepts of equality in sexual relations, the importance of women's relation to other women, and the notion that men and women were born with the same talents. Two-thirds of college women agreed that "the idea that a woman's place is in the home is nonsense," and only one-third felt that having children was an important personal value. Other polls showed similar results, including a rapid change over time. A 1970 survey of college freshmen indicated that half of the men and more than one-third of the women endorsed the idea that "the activities of married women are best confined to the home and family." Five years later only one-third of the men and less than one-fifth of the women took the same position.

Not surprisingly, changing attitudes toward traditional roles in the home were accompanied by shifting expectations about careers. In the 1970 survey of freshmen, males out-numbered females 8 to 1 in expressing an interest in the traditionally "masculine" fields of business, engineering, medicine, and law. By 1975, in contrast, the ratio was down to 3 to 1. In the same period, moreover, the number of women expecting to enter the "feminine" fields of elementary and secondary school teaching plummeted from 31 per cent to 10 per cent. Indicative of the general trend was one survey of eight colleges in 1973 which showed that 82 per cent of the women considered a career very important or important to their self-fulfillment, while only 67 per cent put marriage in the same category. Although such survey data described theoretical expectations rather than actual behavior, the evidence suggested that many women were following through on their announced intentions. The proportion of women in the entering classes of law school skyrocketed by 300 per cent from 1969 to 1974, and many law schools anticipated that women would make up half of each class by 1980. Women doctorates also increased significantly, with the share of Ph.D.'s earned by women growing from 11 per cent in 1970 to 21 per cent in 1975. Although working-class and older women did not share completely all the new ideas, they too seemed to be undergoing change. Non-college young women were less convinced of the value of sisterhood or the reality of discrimination than college women, but the Yankelovich survey showed them endorsing feminist ideas on greater equality in family decision-making, women's right to sexual pleasure, and skepticism toward the traditional homemaker ideal. Older women, in turn, displayed their involvement in change by enrolling in growing numbers in continuing education programs and seeking graduate training for new careers.[15]

The exact nature of the change that had taken place was not easy to define. At its roots, it was a shift of consciousness, a new awareness or sensibility among women about women, and about their relation to men. The consciousness surfaced to some extent in public opinion polls, but it also appeared frequently in more personal and direct encounters—in the comment of a middle-aged woman who said in a phone conversation, "I'll have to check with my

husband," and then felt called upon to add: "We're a traditional couple." Or in the remark of a young woman, not an
active feminist, who was angered because the epilogue to the
film *American Graffiti* ignored women: "Why did they tell us
just what happened to the boys ten years later. What about
the girls?" Or finally, in the bitter comment of a forty-year-
old mother: "I need to be recycled, only no one wants to give
me the chance. I gave away my career fifteen years ago when I
dropped out of graduate school to stay home with the kids."

There was no way to quantify such consciousness, or to
know with certainty what it meant. Yet it seemed to be a
palpable reality—taking root, growing, spreading. It appeared in public school brochures where the traditional "he"
as the description for everyone was replaced with "he or she."
In offices it sometimes blossomed when male bosses, without
thinking, automatically assumed that the "girls" would get
coffee or buy a Christmas present for a female relative. And
in discussions of rape, gynecological practices, who would
watch the children, drive the car, or fold the laundry, it
could suddenly emerge. Wherever the consciousness appeared, change began to occur because in one way or another,
every activity of the day, from interaction with co-workers to
reading a night-time story to children, took on a new significance. Social revolutions, to be sure, do not develop full
blown from the simple emergence of a new idea. Yet heightened awareness of a set of social conditions is a prerequisite
for a change in values, and it seemed likely that as consciousness of sex role stereotyping and discrimination mounted,
other social relationships would be cast in a new light also,
sparking a rethinking process about one's entire life—work,
family, spouse, children, and friends.

Much of the change that had taken place, of course, could
be traced to non-ideological forces. Long-term trends in the
economy, demographic patterns, and cultural values all contributed substantially. In addition, only a relatively small
proportion of the total female population participated, either
directly or indirectly, in the women's movement. If a majority identified with some feminist ideas, only a few were activists. Indeed, many of those who were involved in changing

their own lives might have done so regardless of the movement, as a natural byproduct of the underlying changes in
the society and economy.

Yet the women's movement of the 60's and 70's seems, on
balance, to have been decisive to the heightened consciousness of the younger generation. Behavioral change, prompted
by impersonal social forces, can go only so far. At some point
ideological forces must intervene to spur a transformation of
the values which help to shape and define behavioral options.
In the late 60's and 70's the woman's movement provided
such a spur, criticizing the assumptions, values, and images
that had prevailed in the past and offering an alternative
vision of what might prevail in the future. Although most
men and women did not align themselves vigorously on the
side of feminism, political discussions, media coverage, decisions on public school curriculum, employment practices,
and the dynamics of family living all reflected the impact of
the movement's existence. It had raised questions, presented
demands, and introduced ideas which compelled discussion.
And even when the discussion was hostile, people were considering issues central to self and society in a way that had
not happened before.

VI.

Where Do We Go From Here? Reflections on Equality Between the Sexes

. . . this kind of growing never comes easy.

David Steinberg

By the middle of the 1970's it seemed clear that changes in behavior and attitudes among American women would continue to shape the social history of the country for the remainder of the 20th century. Although no single cause could be identified as decisive to the change, a constellation of social and economic forces had come together, each reinforcing the others, to create a total pattern that ensured an ongoing transformation of woman's "place."

The birthrate continued to fall, each year setting a new record low. By 1975 the fertility rate of women 15 to 44 years old was only half of what it had been twenty years earlier.

This decline, in turn, coincided with a trend toward later marriages. By 1971 more than half of all women twenty years of age were single in contrast to only one-third in 1960, and the number of unmarried women in the 20-to-24 age bracket had climbed from 28 per cent in 1960 to 37 per cent a decade later.

Simultaneously, the greatest increase in the female labor force occurred among younger women of childbearing age. The proportion of women working in the 20-to-24-year-old age group increased from 50 per cent in 1964 to 61 per cent in 1973. Among college women in that age group the employment rate was 86 per cent. But the fastest rise of all took place among women with young

children. From 1959 through 1974 the employment rate of mothers with children under three
more than doubled, from 15 to 31 per cent, and
that for mothers of children three to five years old
increased from 25 to 39 per cent.*

Fourth, poll data as well as professional school
applications suggested a new commitment on the
part of women college graduates to carve out careers, and to view family life as only one part of
their multiple interests. Between 1968 and 1980
the number of women college graduates was expected to increase by two-thirds (twice the rate of
increase for men), providing a growing pool of potential career women.

Finally, the woman's movement continued to
register a significant impact on the expressed values
of young people, men as well as women, creating
almost a cultural consensus that "equality" between the sexes was a good thing. A Roper poll
which showed women supporting the movement
toward equality also showed a majority of men endorsing change. Indeed, one survey of college students indicated that 86 per cent of men, as well as
92 per cent of women, believed fathers should
spend as much time as mothers in bringing up
their children.[1]

As each of these variables interacted with the others, they
created a "multiplier effect," with shifting values and chang-

* In fact, there appears to have been a simple cultural logic at work in
the employment patterns of women since World War II. Those who first
broke the barriers against married women's employment were middle aged.
With no children in the home, they posed the least threat to traditional
ideas of women's "place" as homemakers and mothers. Later, a major
increase in employment occurred among mothers with children six to
seventeen years of age. By the late 60's, in turn, the major change took
place among mothers of younger children. It was almost as though each
step in the process was necessary to prepare the way for the next one, until
by the mid-70's there was a consistent departure from the traditional norm
of mothers staying at home full time to care for children.

ing social and economic conditions building upon each other to produce new patterns of family and work life. By the mid-70's the shape of women's participation in the labor force had come close to matching that of men, and in some age groups, despite a lengthy recession, women's employment had already exceeded the Department of Labor's 1970 projections for the year 1990. Fewer children, a tendency toward later marriage, greater commitment to personal career fulfillment, and at least verbal acknowledgment of the value of equality, all appeared to have created a situation where radically different styles of male-female interaction were possible. Looking ahead, Alice Rossi predicted that "with a longer period of independence socially and sexually [among women], and higher levels of educational attainment and work experience, there may be greater retention of egalitarian sharing in marriages. . . ." [2]

Yet if equality ranked high on the agenda of popular discussion for the first time, it seemed premature to be optimistic about achieving feminist goals. The actual earnings of women had declined relative to men. Although some barriers to equal opportunity in higher education had been eliminated through HEW enforcement proceedings, most patterns of discrimination remained intact. In addition, cultural presumptions about woman's "place" continued to pervade the society. Perhaps most important, there had been little effort to identify or come to grips with the barriers in the way of achieving equality. Americans had a long tradition of describing their political and social objectives in noble slogans, with little attention devoted to the process of implementation. From "immediate emancipation" of slaves to "making the world safe for democracy," the rhetoric of change had been accompanied by a failure to think through the steps necessary to achieve it. Now, the issue of sex equality was in the same position. What did equality mean? How was it to be achieved? What were the institutional and personal changes that would have to take place if men and women were to participate in the condition of equality instead of just talking about it?

If such questions proved difficult to answer, they nevertheless highlighted critical problems that promised to confront anyone interested in achieving equality. The questions were particularly relevant to the young, affluent college graduates who on public opinion polls appeared as converts to the norm of egalitarian relationships, and who were in a situation more conducive than most to the development of new modes of male-female interaction. Not surprisingly, each of the major issues—how to define equality, whether institutional methods for facilitating it could be developed, and how to make it a reality in personal relationships—was tied inextricably to the rest. In the end it seemed likely that the goal could be reached only if a reciprocal process of change occurred, with personal decisions affecting institutional arrangements, and both helping to create a new vision of what relations between the sexes might become.

The basic issue, of course, was how equality was defined. For two hundred years the word had been associated almost indistinguishably with liberty and freedom as part of the American creed. Most Americans saw no contradiction between the concepts, believing that they were encompassed by the overall idea of "equality of opportunity." Thus, although the Declaration of Independence asserted that "all men are created equal," it spoke primarily of the right of individuals to pursue their aspirations without undue interference. No mention was made of sharing wealth, power, or resources. Thomas Jefferson pinpointed the irony of this notion of equality when he described the "natural aristocracy" which would evolve in the new country, based upon each person having the same opportunity to maximize his talents.

Historically, therefore, the idea of equality in America has meant procedural rights rather than the substantive sharing of resources. Through most of the 19th and 20th centuries, the twin notions of legal rights and "equality of opportunity" continued to define the country's perception of equality. As David Potter brilliantly pointed out in *People of Plenty,* simultaneous belief in the otherwise contradictory values of equality and individualism was made possible by America's abundance. As long as the pie of wealth was thought to be infinite, there was no reason why upward mobility for one individual or group should come at the expense of another individual or group. Thus, in theory at least, unlimited opportunity offered the promise that each person could have an equal chance to advance in a society which would remain free of class rigidity or conflict.[3] If injustice existed, it could be remedied by ensuring the aggrieved equal rights under the law, and thereby equal access to the opportunity structure.*

Nothing illustrated the power of this traditional consensus better than the extent to which protestors accepted it. Although some effort was made to redistribute land to ex-slaves after the Civil War, most black leaders concentrated on civil rights legislation and the acquisition of fundamental guarantees of citizenship. The modern civil rights movement continued the same theme, insisting that blacks have the same access to public accommodations and the voting booth as white Americans. As a result, from Montgomery to Selma, black demonstrators emphasized a view of equality that was essentially negative: the *removal* of barriers to citizenship based on race, the *end* of discrimination, the *eradication* of legal impediments to freedom. In a similar way, women activists also focused on legal rights and opportunities. As soon as formal barriers based on sex were eliminated, it was believed, women would be able to achieve their goals. Hence the Equal Rights Amendment also stated its purpose in negative terms: women were not to be treated differently because of their sex. In both cases, of course, the emphasis on legal rights made eminent sense, constituting the necessary first step toward any other advance. Underlying the strategy, though, was a pervasive assumption that extending legal rights and the franchise to blacks and women conferred equal status upon them, and provided the same access to opportunity as all other Americans enjoyed.

By the end of the 1960's, however, the concept of equal

* In fact, of course, mobility was limited, usually consisting of one step up the occupational ladder for each generation. In addition, women, blacks, and Indians were left out of the system entirely. Nevertheless, belief in mobility was widespread, as was the conviction that some form of equal opportunity existed for most people.

opportunity as traditionally defined had come under increasing attack. In the case of both women and blacks, the attainment of legal rights produced a new awareness of less formal patterns of discrimination which effectively perpetuated the status quo regardless of anti-discrimination statutes. Thus freedom to attend a law school meant little if the best law firms refused to hire women and blacks, or if promotions were partially determined by business lunches at private clubs from which minority groups were excluded. Critics of the traditional norms argued that only if everyone in fact started from the same social and economic place could the idea of equal opportunity retain credibility. As Lyndon Johnson pointed out, it made little sense to talk about equality of opportunity to black people when as a group they stood in the valley looking up, while white people as a group stood on a plateau looking down. Thus it became clear that even the possibility of equal opportunity required positive intervention of a substantive kind and that the laissez-faire premises of the past were inadequate.

Understandably, once the concept of equality began to assume a substantive connotation, fundamental issues of self-interest and cultural values were raised. If affirmative action programs were necessary to guarantee recognition to women and blacks who previously had been excluded by hiring practices, what did that mean for the individual rights of white Anglo-Saxon men seeking employment? If publicly funded day-care centers provided the only means of ensuring that women with children could compete with men for jobs or schooling, what would happen to the traditional family, or the belief that the care of young children should be a private matter, not intruded upon by the state? If such substantive issues were not controversial enough, the problem was compounded by an economy in which unlimited growth no longer seemed an option. When one of every seven jobs was related to the automobile industry, some curtailment of expansion appeared almost inevitable, given limited oil supplies. But if the economic pie was no longer infinite, then the advance of one group could not take place without injury to the interests of another, creating the prospect of significant tensions over how to distribute existing jobs and resources.

The issue of how to define equality thus raised basic and divisive questions about the future direction of American society. Virtually no one was demanding a faceless society where individual differences were obliterated and every person had exactly the same share of power, wealth, and resources. Indeed, most suggestions drew heavily on traditional values. Esther Peterson, for example, described a sexually egalitarian society as one "where no one is forced into a predetermined role on account of sex . . . [and] where men and women have the option to plan and pattern their lives as they themselves choose." But it had also become clear that such a libertarian ideal could become a reality only through significant substantive change involving employment practices, education, family life, the training of children for both nurturant and employment roles, and the development of new cultural values and priorities. In almost all cases such issues called for a political as well as a personal response, posing a fundamental challenge to traditional values of individualism and laissez-faire liberalism.[4]

Nowhere was this challenge more visible than in the nation's public institutions, especially business, labor, government, and the schools. If the goal of equality was to come within reach, active cooperation from such institutions was a prerequisite, especially in developing patterns of employment that would make it feasible for men and women in Esther Peterson's words, "to pattern their lives as they themselves choose." Yet American institutions for the most part celebrated individualism, free enterprise, competition, and winning. Whether or not such institutions would move toward greater support of measures designed to promote equality and collective gains for previously excluded groups was an open question at best.

On the most basic level, the issue centered on whether, and how effectively, government, business, labor, and the schools would implement programs to make real the theoretical commitment to equal rights for men and women. How, for example, would labor and management handle the potential conflict of affirmative action and seniority rights, particularly in a time of recession when the last hired—women or blacks—ordinarily would be the first fired? Although a formula apportioning lay-offs according to a negotiated ratio of workers in different categories was not difficult to envision, the issues of equity and competing constituencies promised to make even the best-intentioned negotiations a subject of controversy.

Similarly, the question of how to interpret affirmative action requirements at different job levels seemed fraught with potential conflict. By the mid-70's most universities and corporations were giving *pro forma* acquiesence to affirmative action, but it was by no means clear that most were embarked on a genuine effort to seek out qualified blacks and females for all positions. Significantly, clerical and lower level management jobs were more likely to show change than top-echelon positions. Some argued that there were insufficient candidates of quality for the higher level positions, and Richard Lester, in a report for the Carnegie Commission on Higher Education, contended that affirmative action would lower the standards of the nation's elite educational institutions by promoting second rate people to the top. On the other hand, there seemed enough examples of first rate people who had been kept at the bottom for years because of sex or race discrimination to call that conclusion into question. Thus the basic issue was whether business and educational institutions, and the people in charge of them, would move beyond minimal compliance with the law to promote change actively, even in the face of strong resistance.[5]

In that context, one of the crucial preconditions for greater equality was the willingness of business, government, and labor to initiate work patterns that would encourage men and women to share employment and home responsibilities. Institutional support for part-time positions offered the most readily available inducement for those interested in exploring more equal home/job arrangements. Even more promising, perhaps, was the notion of "flexi-time," a procedure whereby workers were assigned tasks to complete but given the freedom to choose their own work hours with the stipulation that a core period of time—identical for everyone—be spent on the job. An employee with a six-hour job assignment, for example, might work in two three-hour segments, one in the morning and the other at night, or start early in the morning and forgo lunch so as to finish in time for a family excursion in the afternoon.* The difficulty, of course, was that such arrangements created administrative problems that required considerable imagination and commitment to solve. Many employers viewed part-time workers as less reliable than full-time, and complained about the bureaucratic impossibility of figuring out fringe benefits and vacations. "Flexi-time" procedures posed similar problems of supervision, coordination, and reliability. In addition, neither arrangement seemed particularly applicable to management level positions. Probably most important, widespread experimentation with new work patterns required a belief that different social values were either desirable or potentially profitable, and that, in turn, depended on the wider political context.[6]

The same problem of social values was implicit in the issue of whether the government should support day-care programs. Feminists since the time of Charlotte Perkins Gilman had insisted that some form of child-care arrangements would be necessary if women were to have the same opportunity as men to pursue jobs and careers. Yet government involvement in the issue presumed a social decision that mothers of small children should have the same right to work as anyone else, and that young children could be cared for adequately by adults other than their parents. The evidence seemed to support the argument that children over two flourished in day-care centers of decent quality (perhaps even gaining developmentally over those kept at home); other industrial countries, moreover, were committed to far-reaching programs in this area. The Swedish government, for example, enacted a "parent leave" law that permitted either a father or mother to take six months from work, with pay, to care for a newborn

* By 1976 approximately 1,000 companies and government agencies employing 300,000 people were using some variant of "flexi-time." Nearly 30 per cent of the Swiss work force had such a schedule. One of the results has been lower absenteeism and higher productivity.

infant, and government supported child-care centers were available for children six months and older.* France, in turn, provided day-care for all children over three. Significantly, both countries emphasized the educational and developmental aspect of child care rather than custodial supervision. It was not at all clear, however, that American citizens wished to pursue similar policies, either for the purpose of facilitating greater employment opportunities for women, or creating educationally enriching day-care facilities for small children.[7]

In all of these issues, conflict over social values affected the wider political environment and the readiness of institutions to facilitate the movement for equality. At some point it seemed likely that the courts would resolve the clash between the rights of individuals and the demands of groups for more equitable treatment, at least on the issue of affirmative action. However, the questions of seniority rights, child care, and flexible work schedules were so complicated and volatile that no definitive outcome appeared probable for years. Given the importance of political action and institutional cooperation if practical progress toward equality was to be achieved, the absence of either a consensus on new social values, or institutional support for change, posed a major obstacle to early progress toward sex equality. For that reason the political climate established in the late 1970's and early 1980's was likely to be critical for any progress toward equality in areas covered by public policy.

* The Swedish government was headed during the early 1970's by Olaf Palme, a strong advocate of sex equality. The government urged men to take advantage of the parental leave, though early figures indicated that mothers were the ones primarily involved. Despite Sweden's law making day care available theoretically to all children over six months old, only 25 per cent of children from six months to six years were enrolled in such centers, largely due to an inadequate supply of centers and teachers. In Sweden, as in the United States, most day care occurred in the homes of friends or relatives of workers. During the late 60's and 70's the number of children in nursery schools or some other form of day care doubled in the United States, coinciding with the rapid increase in employment among mothers of young chidren. Information on France and Sweden is taken from the "Proceedings" of an international conference entitled, "Educating Women for Leadership," held by the Rockefeller Foundation at the Villa Serbelloni, Bellagio, Italy, March 24–30, 1976.

Ultimately, however, the future of equality depended as much on what took place within personal relationships as on anything else. Although a reciprocal process occurs between cultural values, social institutions, and individual life choices, any long-range change will eventually be manifested in people's immediate personal decisions. In the case of sex equality, the relevance of external issues to the interior relationship of men to women was direct and immediate. Indeed, the nub of the entire problem was whether women and men—individually as well as collectively—could resolve the historic imbalance of power and opportunities that had existed between them. Thus, as feminists pointed out repeatedly, the personal was political, both mirroring and shaping the entire pattern of male-female interaction. In this respect, it was as likely that what occurred in personal relationships would affect the external environment as that outside forces would determine interpersonal dynamics. Since most men and women continued to participate in relatively stable heterosexual relationships, it seemed that the prospects for equality in those relationships would affect significantly the chances for equality in the society at large.

Within the context of personal relationships, one of the most serious obstacles to equality was the different perspective men and women brought to various stages of life development within the existing social order. Instead of synchronizing over time, the activities and interests of men and women frequently clashed, endangering the possibility of mutual growth, and threatening either a disjunction of career hopes or the destructive repression of personal aspirations. The basis for such a conclusion is found in research tying together specific activities with different life stages. Using an interview sample, the psychologist Robert Gould has determined that people in the age bracket 22 to 28 see themselves as building for the future, both professionally and personally. They strive to establish competence in the "real world," making their mark and preparing the occupational niche that will be theirs for most of the future. The stage beginning with the early thirties, in turn, seems to be characterized by more doubt and reflection, including greater skepticism about one's choice of a marriage partner, as well as, simultaneously, greater absorption with one's children. If the twenties are a time to meet the real world with a flush of enthusiasm, then the thirties represent a period to question, before it is too late, whether the choices were wise.[8]

Within the traditional structure of male-female relationships, unfortunately, such a model of life stages seems destructive of the possibility for growth toward equality. Even within an optimum relationship where both participants took full advantage of the possibilities available during their twenties, the new perspectives and greater doubts of the thirties promised to bring problems. But for most middle-class young adults, other patterns were more likely to prevail. Most young couples had children in their twenties, or, alternatively, saw one spouse making a living while the other (historically the male) secured professional training. In either case, the likelihood of both participants being fully involved in establishing occupational futures was slight, a fact which by itself might be expected to generate resentment in a culture that placed a premium on "making it" early.

More dangerous, however, was the disjunction of interests that was likely to occur when people in a "typical" relationship reached their thirties. If a woman had stayed home with children or put her husband through school in her twenties, she was likely to be starting her own career interests at precisely the time when her husband was beginning to question his marriage and life choices. It was probably no coincidence that marriages involving graduate students suffered severe stress when the student, usually a male in the past, finished a degree, and the other spouse, usually a woman, started a career and asked repayment of the sacrifices she had made up to that point. Thus the structure of options within the existing system of life stages appeared to set marital partners in opposition to each other at a critical moment rather than to facilitate mutual support. A 30-year-old woman starting a career needed emotional reinforcement and practical assistance at home. A 30-year-old man, afraid of falling behind in the first stage of his own career and newly skeptical of his marriage partner, might be reluctant to provide such help. Although historically the victim of such a situation was the woman, another casualty was the prospect for equality in a relationship of mutual growth and fulfillment.*

Directly related to the problem of life stages, and in some ways the source of it, was the fundamental incompatibility of the achievement ethic and the social goal of equality. A number of critics charged that in America the values of individualism, competition, and material success comprised the credo of a civil religion.[9] Not surprisingly, many people brought up on such an ethic felt compelled to beat out every competitor and to make their own advancement an exclusive and paramount concern. The goal of equality, on the other hand, required different priorities, particularly the willingness to place the collective good ahead of individual aggrandizement. Within male-female relationships, such priorities would dictate that each participant curtail individual ambitions so that both could find the opportunity for personal fulfillment. Thus a male junior executive in his early thirties might be expected to cut back his hours, and temporarily his prospects for promotion, in order to care for the children and cook meals while his wife finished law school.

Such a pattern, however, clearly would fly in the face of traditional achievement orientations and signify a major departure in the existing middle-class life stage process. Moreover, the idea of equality required more than a change in achievement motivation alone; it also necessitated a recognition that male accomplishments in the past had been made possible in many instances by a "back-up" system of wifely support—a system which in an equal marriage would cease to exist. Progress toward equality thus entailed a two-level process, with husbands not only cooperating in their wives' aspi-

---

* Conceivably, different circumstances would make overcoming this obstacle less difficult. If children were not present, for example, there would be greater likelihood that both participants in a relationship could engage fully in the "building" activities of the twenties. Alternatively, spouses might pursue their efforts to establish competence in the outside world on a gradual basis, sharing equally in the activities of parenting and homemaking. Either of these possibilities, though, presumed a substantial alteration of social values and economic structures.

rations, but also accepting the loss of an older pattern of complete service to the male career. In such a situation, achievement was likely to remain a viable goal only if it was redefined as a joint enterprise rather than as an individual venture.*

Perhaps the greatest barrier to equality in personal relationships is the culture of masculinity. As Ruth Hartley has pointed out, the pressures on male children to conform to sex stereotypes are even more severe than those on girls, particularly prior to puberty. Boys are taught to win, never to run away from a fight, always to accept a challenge. In situations of conflict, the only honorable course is to battle it out, and give the appearance at least of being tough. Not surprisingly, one widely used personality test rated respondents "masculine" if they wanted to lead a posse, "feminine" if they preferred to read poetry. In such a context, the worst epithet that could be applied to a male was to call him effeminate. No matter how far down the ladder a man was in occupation, physical strength, or toughness, he was still expected to appear strong and dominant in his relations with women. Even if a husband broke away from the stereotype in the intimate circle of his immediate family, he attempted to project an image to the outside world of being in control. In the culture of masculinity, images of power surrounded the male-female relationship, determining its outward manifestations and, at the very least, influencing its inward dynamics.[10]

The "masculine mystique" undercut the prospects of equality in two ways. First, the emphasis on external appearances of dominance made it difficult for men to engage openly in activities clearly at variance with traditional roles. A husband might accompany his wife to the supermarket on weekends, but be reluctant to do all the shopping alone, lest

---

* I am indebted to Anne Firor Scott for many of the ideas in this paragraph. She has suggested that many occupational positions might be jointly held, particularly in politics and education. Nor would such arrangements be without historical precedent. Martha Washington, Scott points out, once wrote Mercy Warren that she could not come for tea because she had to write the General's reports.

others think he was doing "woman's" work. Thus some of the arrangements necessary for achieving equality in personal relationships ran directly counter to the requirements for maintaining membership in the "masculine" club. Second, within the male world itself the concern with appearances discouraged the development of shared confidences that might provide emotional support for breaking out of traditional patterns. Men were expected to talk about sports, work, and women in an atmosphere of camaraderie, but not to share self-doubts, anxieties about sex, fears of death or failure, or concern about finding a better way to relate to family and children. Men could turn to alcohol and find an outlet for rage or sadness, but they were not supposed to break down and cry with a friend. Thus the culture of masculinity functioned with both women and men to obstruct the possibility of equality.[11]

Finally, the continuing absorption of men and women in distinctive parental roles raised at least some question about achieving radical feminist goals in family relationships. In a provocative essay entitled "A Bio-social Perspective on Parenting," Alice Rossi proposed that feminist ideals of raising children in alternative family arrangements with multiple parent figures might be destructive to children, and in contradiction to natural rhythms of mother-child relationships. Using endocrinological studies on women's hormonal response to childbirth as a research base, Rossi hypothesized that traditional maternal-infant intimacy was based on biological ties that gave rise to social patterns of close mother-child involvement. Many other observers, in turn, supported the retention of distinctive role modeling for their children, believing that separate male and female behavior patterns were appropriate and healthy for children to see and emulate. Such arguments, of course, did not preclude the development of greater equality. Rossi's data dealt primarily with infancy and were not intended to counter dual-career families or the use of day-care centers. Similarly, a belief in distinctive male and female parental roles did not amount to support of the "masculine" or "feminine" mystique. Yet both arguments suggested resistance to total change of family traditions, or creation of completely interchangeable male and female roles in personal relationships.[12]

In the end, of course, most of the specific obstacles to equality in male-female relationships intersected and reinforced each other. A woman in a conventional marriage who wished to start a career during her late twenties or early thirties required emotional and practical support at home. Yet a man caught up in the achievement ethic might resist providing such support, and place his own advancement ahead of making it possible for his wife to have a career. Even if a man believed a major change in his own work and home pattern was necessary, there was a chance he would stop short of acting on his conviction out of the simple fear that his male peers would view him as not quite a "man." Such obstacles to equality—together with the problems of finding agreement on what the word should mean and institutional means to facilitate change—provided ample reason to reject easy optimism about quick progress toward feminist goals, and emphasized how difficult and demanding the road to new social patterns would be.

If equality was still far distant, however, enough change had occurred to make the "good old days" of total immersion in traditional roles almost equally far away. In the midst of change, the key question was which direction the society would take and how likely it was that the forces favoring greater equality would prevail. Although much of the evidence highlighted obstacles to equality, there were also trends that seemed more conducive to egalitarian social patterns.

Perhaps the most important of these was the continued movement toward smaller families. Children play a central role in the entire issue of sex equality, constituting both a primary obstacle to it and the greatest hope that it can be achieved. Clearly, the process of bearing and rearing children takes away from the freedom to pursue individual aspirations, even as it provides rewards and stimulation not attainable in any other activity. Historically, the requirements of child rearing have been a significant obstacle to women's freedom to pursue careers. On the other hand, the best hope for equality rests with children who grow up to value individual personalities and to interact with each other free of the impact of invidious sexual stereotypes.

In this context, the long-term decline in the birth rate serves the prospect of equality in two ways. In some cases the absence of children may facilitate a more equal life-stage development between the sexes. This seems particularly applicable to college graduates, who indicate both a high valuation of career accomplishments and a relatively low degree of interest in raising children. The Yankelovich survey of the early 70's, for example, showed that only 35 per cent of college women and 27 per cent of college men perceived having children as an important personal value. Just as important, the fact that people having children intended to limit the number made it more likely that births would be planned so that husbands and wives could incorporate child-rearing within their respective life plans and also have the opportunity to create more equitable means of sharing child care and nurturance. Significantly, children reared in homes where both parents were engaged in outside roles were likely to score lower on sex stereotype scales than those in traditional homes. In both cases, therefore, it seemed that a low birth rate constituted a necessary pre-condition for more equality between men and women.[13]

A second trend potentially beneficial to the prospect of equality was the prospect of more limited economic growth. In the past untempered economic expansion had been seen as both a good thing in itself, and essential to the advancement of less well off groups in the society. As a result of such events as the energy crisis, however, Americans appeared to be developing a new appreciation of limits. A slowdown of economic and technological growth had the potential of cutting two ways, of course; in the past economic downturns had led to campaigns to force women back to the home. On the other hand, the spiraling employment rate of women had continued for so long and been so integral to rising middle-class living standards that it seemed unlikely there would be

any reversal in women's employment pattern. In that event,
it was at least possible that an economy geared to lower out-
put would lead to wider experimentation with part-time employment and the development of family work patterns where
each spouse worked only some of the time.* [14]

A third indication of potentially favorable social conditions
could be found in the results of public opinion polls on attitudes toward achievement and material success. A 1973 survey by the American Management Association, for example,
showed that over 60 per cent of middle-level executives did
not view their jobs as a means of realizing their deepest aspirations, and that 83 per cent of corporate officials purported
to be changing their attitudes toward success—a result which
the *New York Times* traced at least in part to the changed values of the late 1960's. Other shifting perceptions were evi-
dent in the Yankelovich surveys of young people. One poll
indicated that nearly 80 per cent of college young people and
74 per cent of non-college young people would welcome less
emphasis on money within the society. Almost half of all
young people also said that they would give priority to self-
fulfillment over economic security in choosing a job. Although such desires required a supportive political and institutional context to be realized and conceivably would weaken
in the face of a real situation—for example, giving up a well-
paying, full-time job for a more rewarding but less well-paid
part-time position—there seemed some evidence of a willingness to re-examine older values and show greater concern
with the quality of life and interpersonal relationships. [15]

Finally, research into husband/wife relationships suggested
that marriages with de facto equality between the spouses

---

* The notion that limited economic growth could facilitate equality runs
in the face of conventional liberal wisdom. It seems at least possible, however, that a tightened economy might force a choice between conflicting
values which liberals (and others) have managed to avoid in the past. Given
the entrenched position of women in the labor force and the confluence of
other social forces pointing toward changed sex role relationships, it does
not seem inconceivable that a pattern of slower economic growth could
contribute to equality.

tended to be happier than those with an imbalance of achievement on one side. Jan Dizard's longitudinal survey of four hundred university educated couples first married in the 1930's showed that maritial discontent was highest in those situations where the husband achieved the greatest success while the wife remained a homemaker. Marital satisfaction, in turn, correlated with moderate or relatively limited career success for the man together with employment for the woman. (Women who combined marriage and a *career* were rare in that generation, perhaps explaining the absence of large numbers in that category.) Although such findings appear to contradict popular stereotypes of the typical "happy marriage," they seem compelling on reflection. If both partners in a marriage work or remain intellectually active, with neither more spectacularly successful than the other, the relationship is likely to have balance. Where one far outdistances the other, in contrast, there is likely to be isolation, gradual separation of interests, and little chance for equal communication. Thus, most observers would give little chance to a relationship between a $90,000-a-year corporate lawyer (female) and her unemployed bookkeeper husband, believing that he would be overshadowed by her career and become totally dependent on her for status and recognition. Reversing the situation in terms of sex, on the other hand, describes a relationship viewed as the norm by many marriage manuals.[16]

Although the results of the Dizard survey reflected accidental rather than intentional equality, they provided support for the argument that those who sought consciously to achieve more egalitarian relationships might also achieve greater marital happiness. At a time when the divorce rate was skyrocketing, and some blamed the trend on women who had forgotten their "place," the evidence showing a correlation between marital happiness and equality of spouses was significant. On the other hand, it remained improbable that most Americans would intentionally scale down their aspirations or possible achievements for the sake of greater contentment. It was one thing to find oneself in a situation of moderate success, and another to aim for that goal, especially when others might interpret the choice as a cowardly retreat from the real world of competition.

Thus all of the trends conducive to equality depended in the end upon the willingness of individuals or groups to turn them to egalitarian ends and create a public environment hospitable to change. The presence of positive forces meant at least that some additional obstacles had been avoided. A climbing birth rate, for example, would have made it more difficult for men and women to find the time or flexibility to develop their own interests. Similarly, the absence of some readiness to re-examine values would have prevented altogether the possibility of considering ideas of greater egalitarianism. Yet the decisive ingredient which alone could transform potential equality into reality was the commitment of people making a conscious choice.

In that sense, change in individual relationships was crucial to a shift in larger social patterns. Most observers historically have viewed the family as a product of social and economic structures, giving little credence to the idea that changes within the family could operate independently to help change the social system. Yet in feminist theory, change begins with the self. If individuals were able to forge relationships of equality in their own lives, they might be able to provide models encouraging others to do the same and eventually generate pressure for change in external structures as well. Thus an integration of public and private living patterns might provide the chemistry for a reciprocal process of change, social and personal, developing simultaneously. Significantly, feminism was one of the few movements in American history that sought to change the self and the external world at the same time. It was appropriate, therefore, that personal decisions play a central role in determining the fate of progress toward equality.

The first prerequisite for a choice in favor of equality was a collective vision of what equal male-female relationships might involve. As Matina Horner, president of Radcliffe, observed, the possibility of equality depended not only on removing social barriers but also on "the reactions and beliefs that the human beings . . . involved have about themselves and each other. . . . We need a shared vision of the way things could be and of better ways to know and understand each other." Part of such a vision would necessarily include a revised perception of men and masculinity, particularly a willingness to support those aspects of men's personalities that are nurturant, emotional, and expressive as well as those that are assertive and strong. If men provided a community of support for each other in breaking away from the masculine mystique, and women, in turn, showed esteem for men willing to risk such a departure, there was a greater likelihood of a successful transition to new norms of male-female relationship.[17]

Just as important, men and women needed to show imagination and persistence in developing the practical arrangements in their own lives that would make equality a tangible prospect. In most cases, this was likely to involve, either implicitly or explicitly, an understanding by the participants of each other's rights, duties, and responsibilities, including the dividing up of household responsibilities, shopping, child care, social contacts, and pursuit of leisure opportunities. The premise of such arrangements was that careful planning in service to a "shared vision" could triumph over the inherent problems of life-stage conflicts and achievement ambitions described earlier. Nowhere did this premise appear harder to act upon than in finding ways to provide each participant the possibility of meaningful work in the outside world in combination with shared responsibility in parenting and homemaking. The options included part-time jobs or careers, alternating careers (one year on, one year off), or the development of "flexi-time" options where one or both individuals in a relationship could shape their own work life. In such situations, of course, what happened to the quality of life in "non-work time," particularly in child care and in attitudes toward historically maligned activities such as housework, would be just as important as what occurred in the job market. Moreover, the readiness of government or business to respond to such arrangements promised to be critical to their workability. Enough people had to choose such a pattern of living to provide a constituency for change, and external structures in turn had to be responsive to that constituency.

In the end, therefore, the underlying issue was commitment to a collective goal, and a willingness to sacrifice some of the society's deep-rooted devotion to individualism to achieve that goal. The conflict of equality and individualism pervaded every question related to the larger problem, from cultural definitions of equal opportunity, to affirmative action, to the prospect of egalitarian personal relationships. There was no way of resolving the conflict without injury to one or the other ideal. Although opting for equality did not mean eliminating individual freedom, it did require constraints on that freedom and a willingness to place certain collective interests ahead of total personal liberty.

In the society at large a choice for equality necessarily entailed greater intervention in the distribution of resources and power in order to make more feasible the creation of equal opportunity. No longer was it possible to affirm the value of equality of opportunity, literally translated, without recognizing the need to guarantee greater substantive sharing of resources so that equal status represented a condition as well as a legal category. Similarly, within personal relationships a choice for equality presupposed a mutual desire to give up some individual preferences for the purpose of realizing that "shared vision of the way things could be." A decision of one person to set aside his or her personal aspirations for a time so that the other could engage in full-time career preparation presumed that at another time the sacrifice would be reciprocated. Without a commitment to such reciprocity, formal or informal, the norm of equality would remain an empty shell within which exploitation and an imbalance of power could continue.

Yet in the mid-1970's it was by no means clear that the young people who subscribed to egalitarian ideals on public opinion polls recognized the implicit value conflict between liberty and equality. Indeed, as at other times of rapid social change, there was a tendency to equate the two and avoid the difficult choices. Powerful trends within the culture ran directly contrary to the collective political commitment required for equality. "Doing your own thing" had become the cultural watchword of the late 1960's and early 70's, identified in the public eye with greater sexual freedom, experimentation with drugs, "hanging loose" in a quick succession of living situations, or simply taking the freedom to do the unexpected and go off on a "trip," imaginary or real. With some justification, many observers viewed women's liberation as both a primary example and a profound source of this drive toward greater personal freedom. Higher divorce rates, demonstrable changes in women's sexual practices, and a new willingness by women to assert their independence and reject conventional social patterns were all cited as evidence that "doing your own thing" and the cause of women's liberation were intimately connected. Indeed, as we have seen, the woman's movement was directly tied to many of the dominant social and cultural trends of the 60's, using them as a foundation for a collective quest for new definitions of self and patterns of inter-relationship.

Still, the goal of equality was both different from and inconsistent with the ethos of individualism and libertarianism. It presumed a willingness of people to subscribe to a collective ideal and work toward building structures within which individuals could derive the benefits of equality. In contrast, individualism presumed acting on one's own desires as a first priority, with collective interests as a secondary concern. In this sense, the historical context of the 1970's resembled in some ways the situation of the 1920's. At that time, another group of "liberated women," the flappers, were viewed as harbingers of a new era of equality because of their defiance of traditional standards and their involvement in "personal liberation." Although the same generation rejected a collective effort to secure structural change, many observers at the time identified changes in "manners and mores" (the old term for sexual freedom and diverse life styles) with equality between the sexes. The same possibility of mislabeling existed in the 1970's if the cause of equality between the sexes continued to be defined primarily in terms of individual liberation. Greater personal freedom was not by itself incompatible with equality, and no one suggested that people repress their basic drive for self-expression in order to continue an "egalitarian" relationship. Yet it was a short-sighted vision that viewed equality as identical only to "doing your own thing."

In the end, therefore, the notion of equality described an entire relationship and could not be limited to personal life style or sexual expression. It was a concept which, if it was to survive, required a context of collective commitment to new values of social interaction. Ideally, the norm of equality provided ample room for individual self-expression and fulfillment. If it did not, the prospects of its winning support were slight. On the other hand, the norm of equality also presumed that self-expression would occur within limits set by the need to give everyone the same opportunity for fulfillment. Only within such a structure could the implicit conflict between individualism and equality be resolved. And only through reciprocity would the goal of equality between the sexes have any chance for realization.

At the very best, then, the prospects for a society based upon sex equality seemed problematic. Not only did the idea of men and women sharing employment opportunities and homemaking responsibilities on an equal basis threaten some of the most deep-seated values of the culture; the notion of equality itself challenged in fundamental ways social, economic, and familial structures based on traditions of individualism and an imbalance of power and resources. On the other hand, the changes already occurring between men and women guaranteed that the future would have a shape significantly different from that of the past. Which direction the change would take was the important question. How it was answered would depend ultimately on a combination of personal value choices, institutional responses, and cultural attitudes. Few decisions held greater importance for the future of American society.

VII.

Epilogue

Although the preceding pages have raised more questions than can adequately be dealt with in this brief concluding word, there are three or four themes that have run through these essays which need to be underlined. The first is the difficulty historians face, methodologically and substantively, in trying to find an adequate definition of women as a group within society. The second, growing out of the first, involves the problem of identifying where women, or groups of women, begin to act collectively in pursuit of a conscious goal either consistent with, or in opposition to, prevailing cultural patterns. The third deals with the enormously complicated problem of discerning how change occurs, and particularly how external, impersonal changes relate to internal, personal responses. The fourth, surrounding all of these, is the difficulty of grasping an issue buried so deep in our social framework and collective psyches that it almost eludes categorization.

It seems logical to assume that the more central a social pattern is to the perpetuation of a way of life, the more difficult will be the process of altering that pattern. The history of sex and race as social issues in America bears out that assumption. Both issues have served as departure points for attitudes and behavior that have been taken almost as second nature by the vast majority of citizens. So pervasive have been our assumptions about color and sex that many people have never considered discrimination against blacks and women a significant issue. Instead it was something that went hand in hand with the particular physical characteristics of those groups—hence inherent, a given, not something to think about. When every layer of social experience—from childhood observation of what people did to the distribution of jobs, the availability of educational opportunities, and the images purveyed by the media—simply reinforced the underlying "truth" of social differences, there was little possibility of altering the status quo, or even knowing where to start.

Precisely because of this multiple reinforcement of prevailing social patterns, change—when it occurred—could not be simple, one-dimensional, or quick. In the case of sex roles particularly, a shift in one area of activity might not affect other areas at all or, if it did, only indirectly and after a lengthy period of time. Once the industrial revolution created a social and economic structure in which the basic roles of middle-class white women buttressed the norms governing woman's "place," it became increasingly difficult to disrupt the cycle of control represented by traditional socialization on the one hand and by effective discrimination on the other.

It was for that reason that World War II was significant in the history of American women. It created new priorities sufficiently urgent that the cycle was broken. Starting with the war, enough behavioral change in economic roles took place over a lengthy period that other areas of women's lives eventually reflected the change also. Like an underground fire, the shifts in the daily content of women's lives were part of a process which, though not visible immediately, helped destroy some of the structural supports of the status quo. As the gap between norms and behavior grew ever wider, there developed a basis in reality for a collective effort to challenge traditional views, and in the ferment of the civil rights decade of the 1960's a revived women's movement set out to create a new structure of male-female relationships.

The key to the process of change, however, was the complicated inter-relationship of external and internal forces. Perhaps the best way to conceptualize the relationship is to see outside developments as creating the context within which collective movements for ideological and institutional change

can occur. Many observers, whether historians or sociologists, oversimplify that process, attributing change exclusively
either to impersonal social forces like demographic trends, or
to social protest activities by groups identified with women's
liberation. Instead, the process is reciprocal. Just as systems
of social control operate on multiple levels of mutual reinforcement, so the process of change occurs through a chemistry of synergism, one development feeding into another and
shaping additional behavioral and attitudinal possibilities.

Nevertheless, within the complicated mix of variables involved in the process of change, collective activity is a crucial
if not decisive component. This is so because implicit in the
notion of collective behavior is a vision of what might occur,
of how the world should look at the end of the process. Collective behavior is important, therefore, because it tries to
direct change, to shape it, to transform otherwise neutral
ingredients into ideologically coherent patterns. Indeed, once
the pre-conditions for major social change have come into
being, the depth and effectiveness of collective efforts to
mold change are critical to the final outcome. That is why it
is significant that the women's liberation movement was
one of the few manifestations of 1960's social activism still
flourishing during the second half of the 70's.

Examples of collective behavior among women, however,
seem different from those found in other groups. Although a
majority of women now appear to support the drive for sex
equality, only a small number identify themselves as activists.
Indeed, a strong collective movement of women opposing
change also exists. It would be difficult to find another group
whose history reveals such a pattern of discriminatory treatment, but whose members divide so vehemently over the
quest for equality. Furthermore, although instances of collective activity abound in women's history, especially if one
includes female reform societies, women's church groups, and
women's clubs, it seems that collective activity directed toward the status of women has flourished only in periods of
generalized social upheaval, when sensitivity to moral injustice and discrimination was widespread in the society as a
whole.

This fact, in turn, dramatizes the underlying problem of defining the extent to which women can be described as a separate group within the total society, either in terms of collective self-perception or objective characteristics. Clearly, women have been viewed as a separate category of people within the cultural norms of society. Similarly, there has been a systematic division of labor based on sex, particularly around the experience of child-rearing and homemaking. Yet the differential experience of women in material conditions of life, and in group orientation according to class, race, and ethnicity, tends to undercut the definition of women as a homogeneous, self-defined, and coherent group within the larger society.

Here the analogy of sex and race appears particularly instructive. Although women, like blacks, have been given an ascribed status based on a physical characteristic and have been victims of discrimination and stereotyping, white middle-class women have not participated in the same collective experience of violence, bad housing, poor education, and ghettoization as have blacks. Instead, there have been major differences among women, particularly in group consciousness, collective awareness of oppression, and commitment to change. Thus, while women have been victims of the same forms of social control used to keep blacks in their "place," they cannot be placed in the same category as blacks either in self-perception or material circumstances.

In this context the scholarly challenge of exploring the model of women as a minority group becomes all the more significant. The future insights of women's history may depend on clarifying how and whether women in the past have functioned as a separate entity akin to other minority groups, despite their distribution throughout the social structure. Questions of a separate female culture or sub-cultures, the role of women's institutions as a rallying point for distinctive group identity, the existence of a separate language or linguistic tradition, and methods of socialization transmitting a distinctive group identity, all pose a major challenge to historians. Meeting the challenge, in turn, will require skills and perspectives beyond those of the traditional historian. The anthropologists' participant-observer techniques will be necessary to develop the interior evidence on how institutions like the church group or coffee-klatsch functioned. The sociologists' tools of survey research will be significant in determining whether or not women have had a differential response to political and social issues. And the specialized knowledge of linguists, social psychologists, and psychologists will be helpful in understanding how women interact with each other, how they relate to men, and what forms, if any, their distinctive patterns of communication assume. If these perspectives can be brought together within an historical framework, it may yet be possible to develop the comparative material that will permit historians better to determine where women have acted as a distinctive group and where their involvement in other groups has been more salient.

The minority group model is perhaps most helpful in the emphasis it places on separate institutions and on a distinctive group identity as a basis for interaction with the dominant culture. Those immigrant groups which were most successful developed strong institutions and community supports as departure points for their contact with the outside world. Thus separatism and effective integration were inextricably connected. Not surprisingly, women too have scored the greatest gains for equal rights and social reform when they have created *their* own institutions. Whether these were female reform societies, women's colleges, or consciousness-raising groups, they provided a home base of solidarity and support for carrying on a collective campaign to alter the wider society, offering the "social space" in which women could develop a new image of self and the confidence to act on it. The vitality of these institutions came from the dual experience of being *for* something which others were *against*—hence the spirited camaraderie of the first generation of women college students, or the women in SNCC and SDS.

In the end, however, the minority group model also proves inadequate. Although it raises basic questions which are essential to probing further the relationship of women to other groups, it does not provide a sufficient explanation for the complexity of women's experience, foundering where every conceptual effort to define women founders, on the fact that females are a majority of the population living in nearly constant contact with men. It is this fact which ultimately prevents women from being a group exactly like other groups, and also makes women's participation in social change so difficult to chronicle. Appropriately, both the strength and weakness of women as a force for social change revolves around this paradox. Thus the movement for women's liberation is potentially revolutionary because, like a guerilla campaign, it is decentralized and exists theoretically in every home in the nation. Yet this same dispersion of the female population also prevents the development of a widespread collective consciousness which would unite women behind the same banner. Precisely because most women cannot avoid contact with men, they lack the clear-cut sense of group identification which comes from living apart as a nation, a religious group, or a neighborhood. Yet the same contact with men makes any effort to secure change reach potentially the entire population. The key, then, is the dialectic nature of women's group identity: they are separate, yet diffused through the larger whole; they are distinctive, yet share an identity with those who are their opposites in every group within the society. It is for this reason that building group consciousness is so central to the prospect for any movement toward equality. It is also for this reason that such consciousness is so difficult to achieve and maintain.

If the crucial conceptual issue remains unresolvable, however, the challenge of finding ways to deal with women's simultaneous oneness and diversity promises to be a continuing source of innovation and insight into America's social history. Rather than bemoaning the elusiveness of women's identity as a group, we should perhaps celebrate it as one of the basic reasons that the study of sex roles can be both significant in itself and also a key to understanding the functioning of society at every social and economic level. Indeed, by taking advantage of the conceptual uniqueness of women's "place" in the larger social order, historians can make the study of women's experience both a rich source of insight into society as a whole, and one of the most promising ways of improving and reshaping our understanding of the discipline of history.

Finally, it may be appropriate to make a personal comment on the underlying issues involved in the quest for equality. At stake are profound questions—of power and how it is exercised, of emotions and how they are expressed, of possibilities for self-actualization and whether they are realized. The ramifications of change in sex roles reverberate throughout the social order, from grade school curriculum to national politics to intimate family interaction. In light of the potential consequences of the drive for equality, it seems there should be greater awareness of the pain and anxiety, as well as excitement and enrichment, that change in sex roles can bring. The personal anguish is as likely to occur with women as with men, and its presence should not serve as a reason for suppressing change. But dislocation is part of the process, and sensitivity toward it may enhance the prospect that the end will be constructive and ennobling rather than destructive and bitter.

In addition, it might be helpful to acknowledge more openly the need of most people for structure and stability in their lives. Growing out of the counter-culture, there has developed a feeling among some people that freedom entails the absence of group norms and regulations. But for our own freedom and fulfillment, most of us need a set of relationships with others to whom we are committed and from whom we receive trust and support. The structure may not be that of the nuclear family, but it is likely to be that of some "family" in the generic sense of people who come to live together on the basis of mutual obligations and responsibilities and find meaning in their relationship with each other.

Overall, however, the effort to promote greater sex equality appears to be in the vanguard of one of the most important, potentially beneficial social changes in our history. Looked at from the perspective of unsettled marriages, shaky cultural norms, and difficult personal adjustments, the losses seem great. But the gains are greater when seen from the perspective of greater personal fulfillment and social well-being. At a minimum, progress toward equality will mean eliminating some of the injustice of existing economic exploitation of women. As females gain equal treatment with males both in pay and career opportunities, the collective resources of humanity for coping with disease, poverty, technology, and economic development will be substantially increased.

But the more important benefits are more subtle. In a society where sex equality existed, men and women might each spend more time with children. Fathers could have the opportunity to develop more openly their nurturant role, and find a greater capacity for expressing feelings of sorrow, fear, vulnerability, and dependency. Women, in turn, could have wider opportunities to fulfill their assertive instincts, and to define on the basis of personal choice rather than assigned roles the nature of their relationship to the home, other people, and the world of jobs and careers. Children, most of all, might grow up with a strong sense of being able to become what they most want to be, rather than what the culture says that they should be. Young boys could act on their desire to play fathers to their dolls without being ostracized, and young girls could build tree houses or play soccer without being seen as deviant. Once the invidious stereotypes were weakened, furthermore, it might be possible for boys and girls, and men and women, to choose freely activities formerly associated with the stereotypes, but this time without suffering any of the limitations or inhibitions that once accompanied those activities.

Perhaps, most important, men and women might learn to view each other as individuals, separate and independent of each other, each with the right to self-determination and fulfillment. If people developed the capacity to understand their own complexity and the diversity of their needs; if they acquired the ability to communicate honestly to each other the nature of those needs; and if they were able to work out arrangements by which, living together, they could respect and encourage each other's development, then the potential for human fulfillment and community would be improved significantly.

The problem with social patterns as they presently exist is

that sex stereotyping and restrictive cultural definitions of masculinity and femininity too often impede the realization of that potential. Husbands refuse to encourage wives to go back to school for graduate training because an independent career for the woman might endanger the structure of the relationship and disrupt the man's self-image as authority and breadwinner. Women keep quiet about their abhorrence of male-centered cocktail party conversations because of fear that they will make men unhappy and be seen as stepping out of place. Men fail to confide their anxiety over growing old or losing work lest they appear weak and "unmanly;" and women tighten their dominance over the process of child-rearing, lest control over the women's "sphere" be taken away, too. In each case, acting according to the prescribed cultural role undermines the possibility of honesty in a relationship and creates the danger of making it into a lifeless form.

The values espoused by those seeking sex equality hold out the prospect of something better. Perhaps the vision of autonomy in a world without invidious sex stereotypes cannot be achieved. Certainly the risks are substantial. But historically, the chances for success seem greater than at any time in the past. And socially, the goal seems well worth the effort.

Notes

Chapter 1

1. Although many have commented on the conceptual dilemmas intrinsic in women's history, no one has explored the issue with greater thoroughness or insight than Gerda Lerner. See, for example, Gerda Lerner, "United States Women's History—Some Conceptual Problems," in *Conceptual Frameworks in Women's History* (Bronxville, N.Y., 1976); "New Approaches to the Study of Women in American History," *Journal of Social History* 3 (Fall 1969); "What Next in Women's History Research?" paper presented at the Conference on Changing Commitments of Educated Women, Radcliffe Institute, October 14, 1976; and "The Lady and the Mill Girl; Changes in the Status of Women in the Age of Jackson," *Midcontinent American Studies Journal* 10 (Spring 1969). See also Alice Rossi, "Equality Between the Sexes: An Immodest Proposal," in *The Woman in America*, ed. Robert J. Lifton (Boston, 1965); Alice Rossi, *The Feminist Papers: From Adams to de Beauvoir* (New York, 1973), Carl Degler, *Is There a History of Women?* (Oxford, 1975); Joan Kelly-Gadol, "History and the Social Relations of the Sexes," *Signs: Journal of Women in Culture and Society* 1 (Summer 1976), and Anne Firor Scott and William H. Chafe, "What I Wish I Knew About Women's History," *Proceedings* of the National Archives Conference on Women's History, April 22–24, 1976.

2. One of the problems historians face perennially is whether, in the face of conflicting evidence, to emphasize differences or similarities in a group under examination. In *The Making of the English Working Class* (New York, 1966), E. P. Thompson shows how important it is to adopt a large frame of reference in making that determination. He brilliantly demonstrates how profound were the connections of class in the culture as a whole, and how dynamic the process by which those connections were perceived and articulated, notwithstanding interior divisions. Thompson's portrait of the emergence of collective consciousness over time and in response to particular issues is a great aid in seeking to understand the development of collective consciousness among women.

3. This particular definition of minority groups appears in Louis Wirth, "The Problem of Minority Groups," in *Man in the World Crisis,* ed. Ralph Linton (New York, 1945), pp. 347–50. Probably the best-known development of the minority group theme appears in Helen Hacker, "Women as a Minority Group," *Social Forces* 30 (October 1951).

4. The thesis of a distinctive woman's culture has many advocates. Carroll Smith-Rosenberg's "The Female World of Love and Ritual: Relations Between Women in Nineteenth-Century America," *Signs* 1 (Autumn 1975) presents one of the most effective and provocative historical arguments for that position, though its discussion of a separate female community seems limited to relatively well-off, educated women. See also Kathryn Kish Sklar, *Catharine Beecher: A Study in American Domesticity* (New Haven, 1973); and Gerda Lerner, "Placing Women in History: Definitions and Challenges," *Feminist Studies* 3, no. 1/2 (1975). One of the abiding controversies, of course, is whether a distinctive woman's culture—if it exists—represents an autonomous expression of a generically female experience, or is a product of, and a reaction to, male domination—hence partly derivative in nature. This controversy is relevant to the sex/race analogy explored in chapter three, especially the issue of whether women, like blacks, have a geographically separate and culturally independent collective past.

There is abundant evidence that a strong sense of separate identity, together with institutions that contribute to pride and self-sufficiency, has facilitated the adaptation of ethnic minorities to the dominant society. If a group has control over its own life, it can interact with others from a position of strength and seek accommodation, at least in part, on its own terms. However painful the process of being excluded from a vacation resort because of race, for example, fighting that exclusion will be less difficult if a group has its own resort of equal or greater value. The absence of group institutions and a distinctive sense of separate identity, on the other hand, leaves control of the situation in the hands of the dominant group and invites a strategy of divide and conquer which places the oppressed population at the mercy of its oppressor. For a discussion of the Jewish ethnic experience, see Moses Rischin, *The Promised City* (New York, 1961); Abraham Cahan, *The Rise of David Levinsky* (New York, 1963 edition), especially the introduction by John Higham; and Irving Howe, *The World of Our Fathers* (New York, 1975). On the political importance of self-sufficiency as a basis for negotiating with the dominant society, see Richard Cloward, "War on Poverty: Are the Poor Left Out?," *Nation,* August 2, 1965.

More and more historians are working on women's institutions, including Louise Young on the League of Women Voters; Nancy Schrom Dye on the Women's Trade Union League; Linda Gordon on free love and purity reform groups; Regina Morantz on women's medical schools and health reform societies; Carroll Smith-Rosenberg on female reform societies; Ann

Firor Scott and Patricia Hummer on Troy Female Seminary; Annette K. Baxter on the American Association of University Women; Barbara Welter on the YWCA; and Amy Swerdlow, Gerda Lerner, and Judith Wellman on female antislavery societies.

5. On the ghetto, see Alan Spear, *Black Chicago* (Chicago, 1965); Rischin, *Promised City;* Cahan, *The Rise of David Levinsky;* Herbert Gutman, *The Black Family in Slavery and Freedom, 1750–1925* (New York, 1976), especially chapter 10; and Carol Stack, *All Our Kin* (New York, 1974). For some of the flavor of life in the early years of women's colleges, see Florence Converse, *Wellesley College* (Boston, 1915); Vida Scudder, *On Journey* (New York, 1937); Agnes Rogers, *Vassar Women* (Poughkeepsie, 1940); and Allen Davis, *American Heroine* (New York, 1973). On women's language, see Robin Lakoff, *Language and Woman's Place* (New York, 1975); and Barrie Thorne and Nancy Henley, eds., *Language and Sex: Difference and Dominance* (Rowley, Mass., 1975).

6. Thompson, *The Making of the English Working Class,* p. 9. The literature on social movements and collective behavior is voluminous. Examples of the traditional approach are: Lewis M. Killian, *Collective Behavior* (Englewood Cliffs, N.J., 1973); Kurt Lang and Gladys Lang, *Collective Dynamics* (New York, 1961); Paul Wilkinson, *Social Movements* (New York, 1971); Mayer N. Zeld and Roberta Ash, "Social Movement Organization: Growth, Decay and Change," *Social Forces* 44 (March 1966); and Neil J. Smelser, *Theory of Collective Behavior* (Glencoe, Ill., 1963). For a discussion and critique of Marx's ideas, see Ralf Dahrendorf, *Class and Class Conflict in Industrial Society* (Stanford, 1957). See also William Gamson, *The Strategy of Social Protest* (Homewood, Ill., 1975), for an analysis of the limits of collective behavior theorists. For a trenchant and stimulating assessment of the emergence of collective consciousness among women, see Sara Evans, "Personal Politics: The Roots of Women's Liberation in the Civil Rights Movement and the New Left," Ph.D. dissertation, University of North Carolina, 1976, especially chapter 10.

Chapter 2

1. Margaret Mead, "Sex and Achievement," *Forum,* 94 (November 1935).

2. For women in the Southern colonies, see Julia Cherry Spruill, *Women's Life and Work in the Southern Colonies* (New York, 1972 edition), especially chapters 3 and 4. The best book on the norms of the Puritan family remains Edmund S. Morgan's *The Puritan Family* (Boston, 1944). John Demos's *The Little Commonwealth* (New York, 1970) is also excellent and, together with Philip Greven, *Four Generations: Population, Land and Family in Andover Massachusetts* (Ithaca, 1970), provides an interior view of the

demography and living patterns of colonial New Englanders. The George Fitzhugh quote is from Anne Firor Scott, *The Southern Lady: From Pedestal to Politics* (Chicago, 1971), p. 17. The *Spectator* quote is from Spruill, p. 164.

3. *The Ladies Calling* is discussed in Spruill, pp. 212–15. Barbara Welter's now classic article, "The Cult of True Womanhood: 1820–1860," appeared initially in *American Quarterly* 18 (Summer 1966), 151–74. Patricia A. Graham's insights are contained in "Women in Higher Education: A Historical Perspective," a paper she generously shared with me. The words of Adlai Stevenson and the *Spectator* are recorded, respectively, in Betty Friedan, *The Feminine Mystique* (New York, 1963), pp. 53–54, and Spruill, p. 244. The magazine quotation is from Elizabeth Cook, "The Kitchen Sink Complex," *Ladies' Home Journal,* September 1931.

4. Material on the lives of colonial women can be found in Spruill, *Women's Life and Work;* Mary Ryan, *Womanhood in America* (New York, 1975), especially chapters 1 and 2; Elizabeth Anthony Dexter, *Colonial Women of Affairs: Women in Business and the Professions before 1776* (Boston, 1931); Nancy Cott, ed., *Roots of Bitterness* (New York, 1972); Mary S. Benson, *Women in Eighteenth Century America* (Port Washington, 1966); and Anne Firor Scott, "Self-Portraits: Three Women," forthcoming. The Pennsylvania advertisement is cited in Ryan, p. 32.

5. See Peter Laslett, *The World We Have Lost* (New York, 1965); Joan Scott and Louise A. Tilly, "Women's Work and the Family in Nineteenth-Century Europe," *Comparative Studies in Society and History* 17 (January 1975); Spruill, "Women's Life and Work"; Scott, "Self-Portraits."

6. Scott, "Self-Portrait"; Ryan, *Womanhood in America.* On demographic patterns generally, see Robert V. Wells, "Demographic Change and the Life Cycle of American Families," in *The Family in History: Interdisciplinary Essays,* eds. Theodore K. Robb and Robert I. Rothberg (New York, 1973).

7. Spruill, chapters 11–14, especially pp. 240–43; Ryan, p. 34; Scott, "Self-Portraits."

8. Spruill, p. 45; Morgan, *Puritan Family* and *The Puritan Dilemma* (Boston, 1958).

9. The story of Ann Catherine Green is told in Spruill, pp. 264–65. For further discussion of the relation of ideals, expectations, and reality, see Robert Berkhofer, *A Behavioral Introduction to Historical Analysis* (Glencoe, Ill., 1971).

10. On industrialism generally, see Douglass C. North, *Growth and Welfare in the American Past* (Englewood Cliffs, N.J., 1966); Thomas A. Cochran and William Miller, *The Age of Enterprise* (New York, 1961); Robert Smuts, *Women and Work in America* (New York, 1959); W. Elliott

Brownlee and Mary M. Brownlee, eds., *Women in the American Economy* (New Haven, 1975). See also Rebecca Harding Davis, *Life in the Iron Mills* (New York, 1972 edition) with a biographical interpretation by Tillie Olsen.

11. The statistics are from Smuts, *Women and Work in America.* See also Caroline Ware, *The Early New England Cotton Manufacture* (New York, 1931); Carroll D. Wright, *The Working Girls of Boston* (New York, 1969 edition of 1889 original); Hannah Josephson, *The Golden Threads: New England's Mill Girls and Magnates* (New York, 1949); and Edith Abbott, *Women in Industry: A Study in American Economic History* (New York, 1919). For a recent local study of women and industrialism, see Susan J. Kleinberg, "Technology's Stepdaughters: The Impact of Industrialization Upon Working Class Women, Pittsburgh 1865–1890," Ph.D. dissertation, University of Pittsburgh, 1974.

12. For some representative works on this period, see Eric Foner, *Free Soil, Free Labor, Free Men* (New York, 1971); David Rothman, *The Discovery of the Asylum* (Boston, 1971); Sklar, *Catharine Beecher;* Rosabeth Moss Kanter, *Commitment and Community* (Cambridge, Mass., 1972); Whitney Cross, *The Burned Over District* (Ithaca, 1950); Dwight L. Dumond, *Anti-Slavery: The Crusade for Freedom in America* (Ann Arbor, 1961); and Martin Duberman, *The Anti-Slavery Vanguard* (Princeton, 1965). On the relationship of various of these movements as they affected women, see Regina Morantz, "Health Reform and Women: A Program of Self-Help," Berkshire Conference on Women's History, June 9, 1976; and Carroll Smith-Rosenberg, "Beauty, the Beast and the Militant Woman: A Case Study in Sex Roles and Social Stress in Jacksonian America," *American Quarterly* 23, no. 4 (1971), 562–84.

13. Phillida Bunkle, "Sentimental Womanhood and Domestic Education, 1830–1870," *History of Education Quarterly,* Spring 1974, pp. 13–30.

14. On the Grimké sisters, see Gerda Lerner, *The Grimké Sisters from South Carolina: Pioneers for Women's Rights and Abolition* (Boston, 1967); Anne Firor Scott, *The Southern Lady* (Chicago, 1971); Katharine D. Lumpkin, *The Emancipation of Angelina Grimké* (Chapel Hill, N.C., 1974); and Eleanor Flexner, *Century of Struggle* (Cambridge, Mass., 1959).

15. On the early feminist movement, see Flexner, *Century of Struggle;* William L. O'Neill, *Everyone Was Brave* (Chicago, 1969); and *The History of Woman Suffrage,* 2 vols. (Rochester, 1889).

16. Alice Rossi, "An Immodest Proposal"; and Bruno Bettelheim, "Growing Up Female," *Harper's,* October 1962. For general discussions of late 19th century America, see Samuel Hays, *The Response to Industrialism* (Chicago, 1957); and Robert Wiebe, *The Search for Order* (New York, 1967).

17. On women's education in the 19th century, see Linda K. Kerber, "Daughters of Columbia: Educating Women for the Republic,

1787–1805," in *The Hofstadter Aegis: A Memorial,* eds. Stanley Elkins and Eric McKitrick (New York, 1974); Sklar, *Catharine Beecher;* Mabel Newcomer, *A Century of Higher Education* (New York, 1959); Bunkle, "Sentimental Womanhood, and Domestic Education"; Jill Conway, "Perspectives on the History of Women's Education in the United States," *History of Education Quarterly,* Spring 1974, pp. 1–12; and Roberta Wein, "Women's Colleges and Domesticity, 1875–1918," *ibid.,* pp. 31–48.

18. Quoted in Scott, *The Southern Lady,* p. 73.

19. On Addams, see Allen F. Davis, *American Heroine: The Life and Legend of Jane Addams* (New York, 1973); Christopher Lasch, *The New Radicalism in American Life* (New York, 1965), chapter 1; Jane Addams, *Democracy and Social Ethics,* ed. Anne Firor Scott (Cambridge, Mass., 1964); and J. O. C. Phillips, "The Education of Jane Addams," *History of Education Quarterly,* Spring 1974, pp. 49–68.

20. Florence Converse, *Wellesley College* (Boston, 1915); Newcomer, *Higher Education;* Jessie Bernard, *Academic Women* (University Park, Pa., 1964), especially chapters 5 and 6; Scudder, *On Journey;* and Rogers, *Vassar Women.* Despite repeated efforts at synthesis, historians remain perplexed by the word "Progressivism" and what it represents. In part the confusion reflects the fact that so many people who assumed the "progressive" label were conservative or even reactionary when it came to human rights. To call "progressive" the age which sanctioned the massive disfranchisement of blacks highlights the contradiction. It makes more sense to apply the term "progressive" only to those who advocated social welfare reforms such as abolition of child labor, wage and hour laws, factory safety, the alleviation of poverty, and the spread of human rights to the powerless. Using that definition, a convincing case could be made that women comprised both the leadership and primary constituency of a "progressive" movement.

21. Wiebe, *Search for Order;* David J. Pivar, *Purity Crusade: Sexual Morality and Social Control, 1868–1900* (Westport, Conn., 1973); Josephine Goldmark, *The Impatient Crusader* (Urbana, Ill., 1953); *Register of Women's Clubs,* New York, 1933.

22. Jane Addams, "Why Women Should Vote," *Ladies' Home Journal,* January 1910; Aileen Kraditor, *The Ideas of the Woman Suffrage Movement, 1890–1920* (New York, 1965); Anne Firor Scott and Andrew M. Scott, *One Half the People* (Philadelphia, 1975); Flexner, *Century of Struggle;* Mildred Adams, *The Right To Be People* '(New York, 1967).

23. For an elaboration of the material presented here, see William H. Chafe, *The American Woman: Her Changing Social, Political and Economic Roles, 1920–1970* (New York, 1972), especially chapters 2 through 4. See also Bernard, *Academic Women;* Scudder, *On Journey;* Graham, "Women in Higher Education: A Historical Perspective"; Adams, *The Right To Be People;* and Virginia Gildersleeve, *Many a Good Crusade* (New York, 1954). A

recent dissertation on the 1920's generally is Alice Shrock, "Feminists, Flappers and the Maternal Mystique: Changing Conceptions of Women and Their Roles in the 1920's," University of North Carolina, 1974.

24. See Chafe, chapters 2 and 3; Janet Hooks, "Women's Occupations Through Seven Decades," *Women's Bureau Bulletin* no. 232 (Washington, D.C., 1951); "The Occupational Progress of Women, 1910 to 1930," *Women's Bureau Bulletin* no. 104 (Washington, D.C., 1933); Sophonisba Breckinridge, "The Activities of Women Outside the Home," in President's Committee on Recent Social Trends, *Recent Social Trends in the United States* (New York, 1933); and Willystine Goodsell, "The Educational Opportunities of American Women—Theoretical and Actual," *Annals* of the American Academy of Political Science, May 1929.

25. Goodsell, "The Educational Opportunities of American Women"; Marguerite Zapoleon, "Education and Employment Opportunities for Women," *Annals,* May 1929; Hooks, "Women's Occupations."

26. Marion Bonner, "Behind the Southern Textile Strikes," *Nation,* October 2, 1929; "Women in the Economy of the United States," *Women's Bureau Bulletin* No. 125 (Washington, D.C., 1937); Women's Bureau, "Earnings of Professional Workers," Women's Bureau Archives, folder entitled "Earnings and Wages, Annual Wages," National Archives; American Association of University Women Press Release on Equal Pay, February 10, 1938, AAUW Papers, Schlesinger Library, folder 54; "The Share of Wage-Earning Women in Family Support," *Women's Bureau Bulletin* No. 30 (Washington, D.C., 1923); and Mary Winslow, "Married Women in Industry," *Women's Bureau Bulletin* No. 38 (Washington, D.C., 1924).

27. Goodsell, "The Educational Opportunities of American Women"; Florence Lowther and Helen Downes, "Women in Medicine," *Journal of the American Medical Association,* October 13, 1945; "Bar Women," *Time,* May 24, 1937; Chase Going Woodhouse, "The Status of Women," *American Journal of Sociology* 35 (May 1930); "To the Executive Board of the National Women's Trade Union League from Elizabeth Christman, Jo Coffin and Ethel Smith," August 25, 1921, Raymond Robins Papers, Wisconsin Historical Society; Benjamin Stolberg, *Tailor's Progress* (New York, 1942); Rose Pesotta, *Bread Upon the Waters* (New York, 1944); Theresa Wolfson, "Equal Rights in the Unions," *Survey* 57 (February 15, 1927).

28. Roger Babson, "Why Women Are Underpaid," *Independent Woman* 11 (December 1927); *Independent Woman* 5 (October 1922); Suzanne La Follette, *Concerning Women* (New York, 1926); *New York Times,* November 17, 1925; Sinclair Lewis, *Main Street* (New York, 1920), p. 85.

29. On changes in sexuality and attitudes toward it, see James McGovern, "American Woman's Pre-World War I Freedom in Manners and Morals," *Journal of American History* 55 (September 1968); Lewis Terman, *Psychological Factors in Marital Happiness* (New York, 1938); Alfred C. Kinsey, *Sex-*

ual Behavior in the Human Female (Philadelphia, 1953). Regina Morantz's "Alfred Kinsey: The Scientist as Sex Crusader," forthcoming in *American Quarterly*, assesses the background and impact of Kinsey's research. See also Guion Johnson, "Feminism and Economic Independence of Women," *Journal of Social Forces* 3 (May 4, 1925), cited in Scott, *The Southern Lady*, p. 230.

30. The Byrd quote is from Spruill, *Women's Life and Work*, p. 81.

31. See Charlotte Perkins Gilman, *Women and Economics*, ed. Carl Degler (New York, 1966 edition of 1898 publication), especially the introduction by Carl Degler; Charlotte Perkins Gilman, *The Home, Its Work and Influence* (New York, 1910); Charlotte Perkins Gilman, "Waste of Private Housekeeping," *Annals*, July 1913; and Carl Degler, "Charlotte Perkins Gilman on the Theory and Practice of Feminism," *American Quarterly* 8 (Spring 1956).

32. Joan Huber, "From Sugar and Spice to Professor," in *Academic Women on the Move*, eds. Alice Rossi and Ann Calderwood (New York, 1973).

Chapter 3

1. Gunnar Myrdal, *An American Dilemma*, vol. 2 (New York, 1944), appendix 5, "A Parallel to the Negro Problem." On the Grimké sisters, see Lerner, *The Grimké Sisters from South Carolina*. A classic statement of the analogy by contemporary feminists is Casey Hayden and Mary King, "Sex and Caste: A Kind of Memo," *Liberation*, April 1966. Helen Hacker's "Women as a Minority Group," *Social Forces* 30 (October 1951) contains an excellent scholarly analysis of the comparison.

2. For a comprehensive discussion of women in relation to the civil rights movement, see Evans, "Personal Politics." *The Black Scholar* 1 (January–February 1970) is devoted to issues revolving around the black woman. See especially Shirley Chisholm, "Racism and Anti-Feminism," and Robert Staples, "The Myth of the Black Matriarchy." The best recent discussion of the sex/race analogy is Catharine Stimpson, "Women's Liberation and Black Civil Rights," *Woman in Sexist Society: Studies in Power and Powerlessness*, eds. Barbara Moran and Vivian Gornick (New York, 1971).

3. Several recent works offer new perspectives on slavery. Among them are Eugene Genovese, *Roll Jordan Roll* (New York, 1974); Peter Wood, *Black Majority* (New York, 1974); John Blassingame, *The Slave Community* (New York, 1972); and George P. Rawick, *From Sundown to Sunup* (Westport, Conn., 1972). On women and the law, see Leo Kanowitz, *Women and the Law* (Albuquerque, 1969). The Stanton quote is from *The History of Woman Suffrage* (Rochester, 1889), and is cited in Stimpson, "Women's Liberation."

4. Stimpson, p. 623. Cynthia Fuchs Epstein, *Woman's Place* (Berkeley, 1971), is an excellent treatment of informal sources of discrimination against women.

5. Barbara Welter, "The Cult of True Womanhood, 1820–1860," *American Quarterly* 18 (Summer 1966), pp. 151–74; Degler, "Introduction," *Women and Economics.* The media provide ample illustrations of the dominant culture's characterization (and caricature) of blacks and women. In the 1950's television series *Life with Father,* Willy, the wide-eyed black yardman, always "messed up," but was always forgiven because, after all, that was the "nature" of happy-go-lucky and childlike blacks. Similarly, Wilma Flintstone of cartoon fame is portrayed as frivolous and irresponsible, even if lovable.

6. For a study of Jessie Daniel Ames, see Jacquelyn Dowd Hall, "Revolt Against Chivalry: Jessie Daniel Ames and the Woman's Campaign Against Lynching," Ph.D. dissertation, Columbia University, 1974, and forthcoming from Columbia University Press. W. E. B. DuBois's experiences are described in *Souls of Black Folks* (New York, 1903) and *From Dusk to Dawn* (New York, 1940). Nathan I. Huggins, *Harlem Renaissance* (New York, 1971), discusses the patron-protégé relationship that often existed in relation to black authors. For sociological insight into the phenomenon of derived status, see Rose Laub Coser, "Insulation from Observability and Types of Social Conformity," *American Sociological Review* 36 (February 1969), 28–39. A classic statement of women's status as derivative can be found in Talcott Parsons, "Age and Sex In the Social Structure of the United States," *American Sociological Review* 7 (November 1942), 604–16.

7. Gerda Lerner, "The Feminists: A Second Look," *The Columbia Forum* 13 (Fall 1970), reprinted in *Decisions and Revisions,* eds. Jean Christie and Leonard Dinnerstein (New York, 1975). For a comprehensive volume on rape, see Susan Brownmiller, *Against Our Will* (New York, 1975).

8. Rossi, "Equality Between the Sexes."

9. Maya Angelou, *I Know Why the Caged Bird Sings* (New York, 1970). For other discussions of black women see *Black Scholar* 1 (January–February 1970); Joyce Ladner, *tomorrow's tomorrow* (Garden City, N.Y., 1971); Carol Stack, *All Our Kin* (New York, 1974); Gerda Lerner, ed., *Black Women in White America: A Documentary History* (New York, 1973); and Toni Cade Bambara, ed., *The Black Woman* (New York, 1970).

10. Angela Davis, "Reflections on the Black Woman's Role in the Community of Slaves," *Black Scholar* 3 (December 1971); Toni Morrison, *Sula* (New York, 1973).

11. Maya Angelou, *I Know Why the Caged Bird Sings;* Mary Helen Washington, ed., *Black-Eyed Susans* (New York, 1975), pp. xviii–xix; Linda J. M. LaRue, "Black Liberation and Women's Lib," *Trans-Action* 8 (Novem-

ber, December 1970); and Bernette Golden, "Black Women's Liberation," *Essence,* February 1974.

12. In presenting what appears to be the prevailing view, Robert Staples has written that "any movement that augments sex-role antagonisms extant in the black community will only sow the seed of disunity and hinder the liberation struggle." See Staples, "The Myth of the Black Matriarchy." The Harper statement is quoted in Stimpson, p. 639.

13. Judith M. Bardwick and Elizabeth Douvan, "Ambivalence: The Socialization of Women," in Moran and Gornick. The argument that blacks had internalized the Sambo image was developed by Stanley Elkins in *Slavery* (Chicago, 1959). Elkins contended that slavery in America was a "closed system" in which blacks had only one "significant other"—the white master—whose authority and cues for behavior they had to accept. The plantation was analogous to the concentration camp, he continued, in the sense that in both places there was no alternative frame of reference from which "inmates" could develop their own values and self-esteem. The problem with Elkins's analysis was that he *assumed* his conclusions— namely, that Sambo was a nearly universal slave personality and that the plantation was a closed system—without ever having examined conflicting evidence. In fact, there appears to be abundant evidence that Sambo was a "role" played on demand, not an internalized personality type.

14. In a brilliant book recently published, Herbert G. Gutman argues that a resilient and vital family network provided the basis for solidarity, self-esteem, and independence within the black community, both during and after slavery. Peter Wood's excellent monograph on black life in colonial South Carolina testifies in a similar way to the strength of black resistance and independence, even in the face of pervasive white power. See Herbert G. Gutman, *The Black Family in Slavery and Freedom, 1750–1925* (New York, 1976); and Peter Wood, *Black Majority* (New York, 1974). An effective refutation of the Elkins thesis also appears in Blassingame, *The Slave Community.*

15. For a discussion of role theory and its significance for behavior and personality, see the following: Theodore Sarbin and Vernon Allen, "Role Theory," in *Handbook of Social Psychology,* eds. Gardner Lindzey and Elliot Aronson, vol. 1 (Cambridge, 1968); Daniel Levinson, "Role, Personality, and Social Structure in the Organizational Setting," in *Personality and Social System,* eds. William Smelser and Neil Smelser (New York, 1963); Herbert Kelman, "Compliance, Identification, and Internalization: Three Processes of Attitude Change," in *Basic Studies in Social Psychology,* eds. Harold Proshansky and Bernard Seidenberg (New York, 1965); Rose Laub Coser, "Insulation from Observability and Types of Social Conformity"; and Seymour Lieberman, "The Effects of Changes in Roles in the Attitudes of Role Occupants," in Smelser and Smelser.

16. See, for example, Keith Melder, "Ladies Bountiful: Organized Women's Benevolence in Early 19th Century America," *New York History* 48 (July 1967); Phillida Bunkle, "Sentimental Womanhood and Domestic Education"; Regina Morantz, "Health Reform and Women: A Program of Self-Help," Berkshire Conference on Women's History, June 9, 1976.

17. Stimpson, "Women's Liberation and Black Civil Rights."

18. Richard Wright, *Black Boy* (New York, 1937), pp. 48, 52, 150, 157. Quotations used by permission of the publishers Harper and Row, New York.

19. Wright, pp. 65, 150–51.

20. Wright, p. 159.

21. Wright, p. 164.

22. Wright, pp. 127–29.

23. Wright, pp. 139–40.

24. Wright, pp. 147, 153–55, 160–61.

25. Wright, pp. 68–71, 200.

26. Wright, p. 175.

27. Wright, p. 72.

28. Wright, p. 148.

29. Wright, pp. 150–51; Brownmiller, *Against Our Will;* Jerome Kagan and H. A. Moss, *Birth to Maturity* (New York, 1962).

30. Degler, "Introduction," *Women and Economics.*

31. Lewis, *Main Street,* pp. 74, 167; Marge Piercy, *Small Changes* (Greenwich, Conn., 1972), p. 33.

32. Louis P. Harlan, *Booker T. Washington, 1856–1901* (New York, 1972); Ralph Ellison, *Invisible Man* (New York, 1952); Flexner, *Century of Struggle,* p. 33; and Dara DeHaven, "On Educating Women'—The Co-ordinate Ideal at Trinity and Duke University," Masters thesis, Duke University, 1974.

33. Piercy, *Small Changes,* pp. 19–20, 29, 40–41; Lewis, *Main Street,* pp. 14–15, 86, 283.

34. Bardwick and Douvan, "Ambivalence: The Socialization of Women"; Wright, *Black Boy,* pp. 207–13.

35. Piercy, *Small Changes,* pp. 31, 34, 316–17.

36. Piercy, pp. 30–31, 34, 39; Mirra Komarovsky, "Cultural Contradictions and Sex Roles," *American Journal of Sociology* 52 (November 1946).

37. Lewis, *Main Street,* p. 234.

38. Wright, *Black Boy,* p. 199.

39. Wright, p. 172.

40. Wright, p. 144; Lewis, *Main Street,* pp. 404–5; Piercy, *Small Changes,* p. 41.

41. See Everett Hughes, "Social Change and Status Protest: An Essay on the Marginal Man," *Phylon* 10 (December 1949); and Robert K. Merton, *Social Theory and Social Structure* (New York, 1965), pp. 225–50.

42. Wright, *Black Boy,* p. 130; Maya Angelou, *I Know Why the Caged Bird Sings,* p. 3.

43. Vivian Gornick, "Woman as Outsider," in Moran and Gornick, pp. 126–44.

44. Angelou, p. 153.

45. Gornick, p. 140.

Chapter 4

1. On the intersection of political will and social change, see Luther P. Gerlach and Virginia H. Hine, *People, Power, Change: Movements of Social Transformation* (Indianapolis, 1970).

2. See, for example, Carroll Smith-Rosenberg, "The Hysterical Woman: Sex Roles and Role Conflict in Nineteenth-Century America," *Social Research* 39 (Winter 1972), 652–78. The *Fortune* poll is reported in "Fortune Survey: Women in America," *Fortune,* August 1946, pp. 5–6.

3. On the 1930's, see Harvard Sitkoff, "Race Relations: Progress and Prospects," in *Paths to the Present,* ed. James T. Patterson (Minneapolis, 1974); Robert L. Zangrando, "The NAACP and a Federal Anti-Lynching Bill, 1934–1940," *Journal of Negro History* 50 (April 1965), 106–17; John B. Kirby, "The Roosevelt Administration and Blacks: An Ambivalent Legacy," in *Twentieth Century America: Recent Interpretations,* eds. Barton Bernstein and Allan Matusow (New York, 1972); Leslie Fishel, "The Negro in the New Deal Era," *Wisconsin Magazine of History* 48 (Winter 1964–65), 111–23; and Joseph Lash, *Eleanor and Franklin* (New York, 1973).

4. See Jervis Anderson, *A. Philip Randolph* (New York, 1973); Richard Dalfiume, "The Forgotten Negro Revolution," reprinted in *The Shaping of Twentieth Century America,* eds. Richard Abrams and Lawrence Levine (Boston, 1971); Harvard Sitkoff, "Racial Militance and Interracial Violence in the Second World War," *Journal of American History* 58 (December 1971), 661–81.

5. The information in these paragraphs is drawn from Sitkoff, "Race Relations"; Dalfiume, "The Forgotten Negro Revolution"; Sitkoff, "Racial Militance and Interracial Violence"; Herbert Garfinkel, *When Negroes March* (Glencoe, Ill., 1959); and Richard Dalfiume, *Desegregation of the U.S. Armed Forces: Fighting on Two Fronts, 1939–1953* (Columbia, S.C., 1969).

6. Dalfiume, *Desegregation;* Harvard Sitkoff, "Harry Truman and the Election of 1948: The Coming of Age of Civil Rights in American Politics," *Journal of Southern History* 37 (November 1971), 597–616; William Berman, *The Politics of Civil Rights in the Truman Administration* (Columbus, Ohio, 1970); Donald McCoy and Richard Ruetta, *Quest and Response* (Lawrence, Kansas, 1973); and Barton J. Bernstein, "The Ambiguous Legacy: The Truman Administration and Civil Rights," in *Politics and Policies of the Truman Administration,* ed. Barton Bernstein (Chicago, 1970), pp. 269–314.

7. Richard Kluger, *Simple Justice: The History of Brown v. Board of Education and Black America's Struggle for Equality* (New York, 1976); Albert P. Blaustein and Clarence C. Ferguson, Jr., *Desegregation and the Law* (New York, 1962); Melvin Tumin, *Desegregation* (Princeton, 1957); and Allan Wolk, *The Presidency and Black Civil Rights* (Rutherford, N.J., 1971).

8. Herman P. Miller, *Rich Man, Poor Man* (New York, 1971).

9. Martin Luther King, Jr., *Stride Toward Freedom* (New York, 1958); Howard Zinn, *The Southern Mystique* (New York, 1964); Howard Zinn, *SNCC: The New Abolitionists* (Boston, 1965); Benjamin Muse, *The American Negro Revolution* (New York, 1968); Louis Lomax, *The Negro Revolt* (New York, 1962); and William H. Chafe, "Greensboro: A Case Study of Social Change in Race Relations," forthcoming.

10. Allan Matusow, "From Civil Rights to Black Power: The Case of SNCC, 1960–1966," in Bernstein and Matusow; Reese Cleghorn and Pat Watters, *Climbing Jacob's Ladder* (New York, 1965); Muse, *The American Negro Revolution;* Vincent Harding, "Black Radicalism: The Road from Montgomery," in *Dissent: Explorations in the History of American Radicalism,* ed. Alfred Young (DeKalb, Ill., 1968).

11. Stokely Carmichael and Charles Hamilton, *Black Power: The Politics of Liberation* (New York, 1967); Carmichael, "What We Want," *New York Review of Books,* September 22, 1966; Carmichael, "Toward Black Liberation," *Massachusetts Review* 7 (Autumn 1966); Julius Lester, *Look Out Whitey! Black Power's Gon' Get Your Mama* (New York, 1968); Bayard Rustin, "From Protest to Politics; The Future of the Civil Rights Movement," *Commentary,* February 1965; and Harold Cruse, *The Crisis of the Negro Intellectual* (New York, 1967). For a discussion of the white response, see Angus Campbell, *White Attitudes Toward Black People* (Ann Arbor, 1971); Murray Friedman, ed., *Overcoming Middle-Class Rage* (New York, 1972); and Richard Lemon, *The Troubled Americans* (New York, 1970).

12. Material for this section is drawn from Chafe, *The American Woman,* especially chapters 6–8. See also Katherine Glover, *Women at Work in Wartime* (Washington, D.C., 1943); International Labor Organization, *The War and Women's Employment* (Montreal, 1946); Florence Cadman, "Womanpower 4 F," *Independent Woman* 22 (September 1943); Helen Baker, *Women in War Industries* (Princeton, 1942); and "More Child Care," *Business Week,* August 26, 1944.

13. "Women Workers in Ten Production Areas and Their Postwar Employment Plans," *Women's Bureau Bulletin* no. 209 (Washington, D.C., 1946); and "Give Back Their Jobs," *Woman's Home Companion,* October 1943.

14. Frances Levison, "What the Experts Say," *Life,* June 16, 1947; Perry Bruton, "Present-Day Thinking on the Woman Question," *Annals* 251 (May 1947); Agnes Meyer, "Women Aren't Men," *Atlantic,* August 1950; National Manpower Council, *Womanpower* (New York, 1955); Elizabeth Baker, *Technology and Woman's Work* (New York, 1964); National Manpower Council, *Work in the Lives of Married Women* (New York, 1957); Elizabeth Waldman, "Changes in the Labor Force Activity of Women," *Monthly Labor Review* 93 (June 1970).

15. Women's Bureau Memorandum, August 22, 1945, Women's Bureau Archives; "Fortune Survey: Women in America," *Fortune,* August 1946; Valerie K. Oppenheim, *The Female Labor Force in the United States* (Berkeley, 1970).

16. For a comprehensive summary of the sociological research in this area, see Lois N. Hoffman and Francis Nye, eds., *The Employed Mother in America* (Chicago, 1963); and Lois N. Hoffman, Francis Nye, and Stephen J. Baker, eds., *Working Mothers* (San Francisco, 1974).

17. Material for this section is drawn from Jo Freeman, *The Politics of Women's Liberation* (New York, 1975); Evans, "Personal Politics"; Chafe, *The American Woman,* chapter 10. See also Maren Lockwood Carden, *The New Feminist Movement* (New York, 1974); Judith Hole and Ellen Levine, *The Rebirth of Feminism* (New York, 1971); Lerner, "The New Feminism: A Second Look"; Peter G. Filene, *Him, Her, Self* (New York, 1974); Robin Morgan, ed., *Sisterhood Is Powerful* (New York, 1970); Elizabeth Janeway, *Man's World, Woman's Place* (New York, 1971); and Piercy, *Small Changes.*

18. For another discussion of the influence of cultural contradictions on emerging consciousness, see Nancy McWilliams, "Contemporary Feminism, Consciousness-Raising, and Changing Views of the Political," in Jane Jacquette, *Women in Politics* (New York, 1974).

19. In *Democratic Promise: The Populist Movement in America* (New York, 1976), Lawrence Goodwyn argues that every insurgent movement involves the discovery of new forms of expression which, in turn, come to symbolize

the perception of reality that is the movement's essence. For the Populists, that form of expression was the cooperative movement where farmers created both a means of fighting finance capitalism and an institution for affirming their solidarity. In the process, they came to see themselves and their world in a new light. The cooperative crusade thus embodied what Goodwyn calls the "movement culture"—its distinctive values and the organizational framework within which it sought change. Sara Evans develops a similar idea in her discussion of women's liberation.

The argument being made here is that both the sit-in and the consciousness-raising session provided those "new forms of expression" through which insurgent blacks and women articulated a different vision of reality and acted to achieve it. I am indebted to Lawrence Goodwyn especially, and to Sara Evans and Harry Boyte, for their insights in this area.

20. Lerner, "The New Feminism: A Second Look"; and Evans, "Personal Politics," especially chapter 10.

21. For further discussion of Perkins's ideas, see Chafe, *The American Woman*, pp. 107, 110.

22. Epstein, *Woman's Place*.

23. Catharine Stimpson, " 'Thy Neighbor's Wife, Thy Neighbor's Servants': Women's Liberation and Black Civil Rights," in Moran and Gornick, p. 651.

24. Anne Firor Scott, *The Southern Lady: From Pedestal to Politics* (Chicago, 1971); Hall, "Revolt Against Chivalry."

25. Hall, chapter 4.

26. Evans, "Personal Politics"; Richard Gillam, "White Racism in the Civil Rights Movement," *Yale Review* 62 (Summer 1973), 520–43.

27. Evans, "Personal Politics"; and Casey Hayden and Mary King, "Sex and Caste: A Kind of Memo," *Liberation*, April 1966.

Chapter 5

1. On the political impact of the suffrage, see Chafe, *The American Woman*, chapter 1. See also, Emily Newell Blair, "Are Women a Failure in Politics?" *Harper's*, October 1925; Stuart H. Rice and Malcolm Willey, "American Women's Ineffective Use of the Vote," *Current History* 20 (July 1924); and Susan Tolchin and Martin Tolchin, *Clout* (New York, 1974).

2. Mildred Adams, *The Right To Be People* (New York, 1967); Degler, "Introduction," in *Women and Economics;* Afred Kinsey, *Sexual Behavior*, especially pp. 422–23.

NOTES   3. For further discussion of some of these ideas, see Chafe, *The American Woman,* chapters 7–10. Footnote 14 in this chapter cites public opinion polls over the past two decades. On working women's response, see Patricia Cayo Sexton, "Workers (Female) Arise!," *Dissent,* Summer 1974, pp. 380–95.

4. "Birth Dearth," *Christian Century,* November 24, 1971; "End of Baby Boom," *Scientific American,* April 1968; "Z.P.G.," *Scientific American,* April 1971; Lawrence A. Mayer, "Why the U.S. Population Isn't Exploding," *Fortune,* April 1967; Conrad Taueber, "Population Trends and Statistics," in *Indicators of Social Change,* eds. Eleanor B. Sheldon and Wilbert E. Moore (New York, 1968); Miller, *Rich Man, Poor Man; New York Times,* November 5, 1971, February 22, 1972; Alice Rossi, "Social Trends and Women's Lives, 1965 to 1985," paper presented at the Rockefeller Foundation Conference on "Educating Women for the Future," March 24–30, 1976.

5. Robert K. Bell and Jay B. Clarke, "Pre-marital Sexual Experience Among Coeds, 1958 and 1968," *Journal of Marriage and the Family* 32 (February 1970), 81–84; American Council of Education, *The American Freshman: National Norms for Fall, 1975* (New York, 1976) cited in Rossi "Social Trends"; Joseph Katz, "Evolving Relationships Between Women and Men," paper presented at the Rockefeller Foundation Conference on "Educating Women for the Future"; Joseph Katz, "Coeducational Living: Effects Upon Male-Female Relationships," in *Student Development and Education in College Residence Halls,* eds. David A. DeCoster and Phyllis L. Mable (Washington, D.C., 1974); P. Sorensen, *Adolescent Sexuality in Contemporary America* (New York, 1973); and Daniel Yankelovich, *The New Morality: A Profile of American Youth in the 70's* (New York, 1974), especially chapters 8 and 9.

6. On the 19th-century feminist movement, see Flexner, *Century of Struggle;* and Kraditor, *The Ideas of the Woman Suffrage Movement, 1890–1920.* For the 20th century, see Scott and Scott, *One Half the People;* James Stanley Lemons, *The Woman Citizen* (Urbana, Ill., 1972); and Chafe, *The American Woman.* The contemporary movement is discussed in Freeman, *The Politics of Women's Liberation;* Evans, "Personal Politics"; Carden, *The New Feminist Movement;* and Hole and Levine, *The Rebirth of Feminism.* On the Women's Trade Union League, see Chafe, chapter 3; and Nancy Schrom Dye, "Creating a Feminist Alliance: Sisterhood and Class Conflict in the New York Women's Trade Union League, 1903–1914," *Feminist Studies* 2 (1975), 24–38. For an account of black feminism, see "Black Feminism: A New Mandate," *Ms.,* May 1974. CLUW is discussed in Sexton, "Workers (Female) Arise."

7. Jo Freeman, "The Tyranny of Structurelessness," *Berkeley Journal of Sociology: A Critical Review* 17 (1972–73), 151–64.

8. I am indebted to Harry Boyte for developing the ideas contained in this paragraph.

9. For a discussion of the National Women's Party and the ERA in the 20's and 30's, see Chafe, *The American Woman*, chapter 5.

10. George Gilder, *Sexual Suicide* (New York, 1973), especially pp. 257–61.

11. *New York Times*, November 6, 7, 8, 9, 1975; December 8, 1975.

12. This account of the socialist-feminist conference is drawn from three stories which appeared in *Off Our Backs*, August 1975. The stories were written by Madeleine Janover, Fran Moira, and Cathy Heifetz, and to some extent reflect different perspectives. *Off Our Backs* is a women's liberation monthly which provides excellent coverage of many movement activities, especially those of a less "establishment" nature.

13. For a discussion of the Steinem controversy, see *Off Our Backs*, May, July, and September–October 1975. The September–October issue contains Steinem's open letter to women of the movement responding to the charge by Redstockings, a New York feminist group, that she had been a CIA operative. *Ms.* magazine, which Steinem helped to found, was accused by radical feminists of trimming on the issues and caving in to the "establishment." Robin Morgan's "Rights of Passage," *Ms.*, September 1975, is a moving commentary on the conflicts within the movement, as well as an affirmation of feminism's underlying message. Betty Friedan's *It Changed My Life* (New York, 1976) attacks those segments of the movement which she defines as radical, especially lesbian-feminists. For a misanthropic view of all sides of the movement, see Veronica Geng, "Requiem for the Women's Movement," *Harper's*, November 1976.

14. George Gallup and Evan Hill, "The American Woman," *Saturday Evening Post*, December 22, 1962, *The Gallup Opinion Index*, September 1970, Report no. 63; "The Harris Survey," May 20, 1971, December 11, 1975; "The Roper Poll," *New York Times*, October 3, 1974; and Cynthia Fuchs Epstein, "Ten Years Later: Perspectives on the Women's Movement," *Dissent*, Spring 1975.

15. Yankelovich, *The New Morality*, chapters 8 and 9; Rossi, "Social Trends in Women's Lives"; American Council of Education, *The American Freshman: National Norms*, reports from 1970 and 1975 classes; Katz, "Emerging Relationships Between Men and Women"; J. L. McCarthy and D. Wolfle, "Doctorates Granted to Women and Minority Group Members," *Science*, September 12, 1975.

1. Rossi, "Social Trends and Women's Lives; *New York Times,* November 5, 1971, October 3, 1974; "Birth Dearth," *Christian Century,* November 24, 1971; Juanita Kreps, ed., *Women and the American Economy* (Englewood Cliffs, N.J., 1976), especially chapters 2, 3, and 5; Yankelovich, *The New Morality,* chapters 8 and 9; Katz, "Emerging Relationships Between Men and Women."

2. Karl E. Taeuber and James A. Sweet, "Family and Work: The Social Life Cycle of Women," in Kreps; Rossi, "Social Trends and Women's Lives."

3. David Potter, *People of Plenty: Economic Abundance and the American Character* (Chicago, 1954), especially pp. 91–110. For two books that examine social mobility, see Stephan Thernstrom, *The Other Bostonians* (Cambridge, Mass., 1974); and Seymour M. Lipset and Reinhard Bendix, *Social Mobility in Industrial Society* (Berkeley, 1967).

4. The Esther Peterson statement appears in Jessie Bernard, "Changing Family Life Styles: One Role, Two Roles, Shared Roles," in *The Future of the Family,* ed. Louise Kapp Howe (New York, 1972), p. 245. Other salient comments on equality in the same volume can be found in S. M. Miller, "Confusions of a Middle-Class Husband," pp. 95–108; and Olaf Palme, "Lesson from Sweden," pp. 247–60. The debate on equality and egalitarianism has spawned a number of books recently, many arguing against either the possibility or desirability of greater substantive equality. See, for example, Nathan Glazer, *Affirmative Discrimination: Ethnic Inequality and Public Policy* (New York, 1976).

Arthur M. Okun, *Equality and Efficiency, The Big Tradeoff* (Washington, D.C., 1976), takes a middle-of-the-road position. John Rawls, *Theory of Justice* (Cambridge, Mass., 1971), provides a strong argument for more equality. The position presented here is that "equality of opportunity" is a meaningless phrase unless accompanied by substantive measures that assure people a relatively similar starting place. Although critics argue that such change would entail an oppressive bureaucracy that would be destructive of human rights, there seems no obvious reason why a truly progressive tax system and a guaranteed income would mean an increase in government bureaucracy.

5. Richard Lester, *Anti-Bias Regulations of Universities: Faculty Problems and Their Solutions* (New York, 1974).

6. For an excellent discussion of "flexi-time," see Barry Stein, Allan Cohen, and Herman Gadon, "Flextime: Work When You Want To," *Psychology Today* 10 (June 1976).

7. See Lois Hoffman and Francis Nye, eds., *The Employed Mother in America* (Chicago, 1963); Lois Hoffman, F. Ivan Nye, and Stephen J. Baker, *Work-*

ing Mothers (San Francisco, 1974); and Pamela Roby, *Child Care—Who Cares? Foreign and Domestic Infant and Early Childhood Development Policies* (New York, 1973).

8. For a discussion of life stages, see Roger Gould, "Adult Life Stages: Growth Toward Self-Tolerance," *Psychology Today* 8 (February 1975); Jack Block, *Lives Through Time* (Berkeley, 1971); Erik Erikson, *Childhood and Society* (New York, 1950). Gail Sheehy's *Passages* (New York, 1976) explores many of the transitions in adult life. Sheehy uses in-depth interviews to illustrate her findings.

9. See, for example, Robert Bellah, *The Broken Covenant: American Civil Religion in Time of Trial* (New York, 1975).

10. Ruth Hartley, "Sex-Role Pressures in the Socialization of the Male Child," *Psychological Reports* 5 (1959), 457–68.

11. Many recent books have explored the culture of masculinity, and the high price, as well as large rewards, of male power. The best single-volume introduction is Joseph H. Pleck and Jack Sawyer, eds., *Men and Masculinity* (Englewood Cliffs, N.J., 1974). See also Filene, *Him, Her, Self* (New York, 1974), especially chapter 7; Michael Korda, *Male Chauvinism: How It Works* (New York, 1973); and Marc Feigen Fasteau, *The Male Machine* (New York, 1974).

12. Alice Rossi, "A Bio-Social Perspective on Parenting," forthcoming (1977) in *Daedalus*. As she has done throughout her career, Rossi is breaking new ground and raising profound questions central to how equality between men and women within the family might be achieved.

13. Yankelovich, *The New Morality*, chapters 1, 4, 6–10; Nye and Hoffman, eds., *The Employed Mother in America*, especially Lois Hoffman, "Effects on Children: Summary and Discussion."

14. Robert Heilbroner's *Inquiry into the Human Prospect* (New York, 1974) is one of the more controversial assessments of future economic and technological growth. Experts on the economy and world energy resources have questioned Heilbroner's predictions of a crisis if rapid growth continues. They argue that scientific innovation and the discovery of new resources will keep pace with demand. Others have dissented from Heilbroner's conclusion that governmental despotism is likely in a world of diminishing resources. The view expressed here is that changing attitudes toward sex roles, as well as shifting behavior patterns, may produce different cultural values toward individualism and success. In that event, a pattern of limited growth might reinforce, or help call into being, new work arrangements for men and women. It is too soon, of course, to know how likely such an eventuality is, but recent labor negotiations involving the United Auto Workers and the New York City Police suggest a willingness to spread out jobs to more people, even at the sacrifice of wage increases. In short, cur-

rent predictions of disaster from either too rapid or too limited economic growth seem to underestimate the significance of the human response, and the potential for creative adaptation.

15. *New York Times,* June 3, 1973; Yankelovich, *The New Morality,* especially chapters 8 and 10.

16. Jan E. Dizzard, "The Price of Success," in Howe.

17. *New York Times,* July 15, 1974.

Index

Calvert, Leonard, 19
Career women, 18-19, 27-28, 30-31, 68-70, 139-40, 146
Carmichael, Stokely, 91
Carnegie Commission on Higher Education, 152
Carolina frontier, 18
Catt, Carrie Chapman, 38
Chicago, 74
Child labor legislation, 29
Church, as mechanism of social control and social change, 71
Civil Rights Act, 1964, 96
Civil rights movement, 45, 57-58, 81, 89-92, 96, 101, 130-31; effect on women, 96, 102; historic attitudes toward equality, 149
Class, vii-ix, 3, 7, 22-24, 30-31, 33, 35-36, 76
Coalition of Labor Union Women, 125
Collective behavior, 6-10, 36-38, 41, 81-82, 172-74
College women, 26-27, 32-33, 37, 40-41, 70, 146; their sense of mission, 28; attitudes in the 1920's, 29-30; and marriage, 30; attitudes toward feminism, 140
Colonial America, 16-21
Committee on Civil Rights, 87
Committee on Inter-Racial Cooperation, 108
Consciousness-raising groups, 97-98, 103, 131
Crop lien system, 84
Cuba, 137
"Cult of domesticity," 16
Cultural norms, 7-11, 15-17, 20-21, 26, 34-38, 41, 94-95; as opposed to behavior, 15-17, 20-21, 101; the power of traditional attitudes toward masculinity and femininity, 132-33; on equality, 148-50; on individualism and achievement, 151-54, 158; toward men, 158-59

Davis, Angela, 52
Davis, Rebecca Harding, 23
Day care, 39, 93, 150, 153-54
Declaration of Independence, 148
Declaration of Sentiments, 25

Degler, Carl, 48-49
Demography, 17-19, 26-27, 120-21
Depression, 15
Desegregation: of armed forces, 88; of schools, 88-89
Discrimination: informal varieties of, 150; see also Blacks; Women
Divorce, 163, 167
Dizard, Jan, 162-63
Dominant culture: definition of women, 8-9, 38-39; attitudes toward women and blacks, 48-49, 53, 92; rebellion against by blacks, 92, 103-6; rebellion against by women, 98-99, 103-6; definition of equality, 148-51; attitudes toward individualism, 151-53; attitudes toward masculinity, 158-59
Douglass, Frederick, 74
Douvan, Elizabeth, 55, 69
DuBois, W.E.B., 50, 74
Duke University, 68

Economy: family-centered, 9, 16-20, 34-35; women's role in, 9, 16-20, 34-35; impact of industrialism, 21-24, 35-36; employment statistics on women, 23, 30-32, 92-93, 94-95, 145; employment statistics on blacks, 86-87; impact of World War II, 92; limits of growth, 150, 161-62
Education, 9, 26-29; desegregation, 88
Employment among women, 23, 30-32, 92-93, 95, 145, 161-62; among married women, 32-33, 67-69, 92-94, 119-20; among young women, 145-46; among women with children, 145-46; relation to day care, 39, 93, 153-54
Epstein, Cynthia Fuchs, 104
Equality, 25-26, 38-39, 85, 101, 146-47, 177-79; historic definition of, 148-51; role of institutions, 151-54; conflict with achievement ethic and individualism, 154, 157-58, 166-68; difficulty of achieving in personal relations, 155-60, 162-68; obstacle of differential life stages, 155-66; problem of "masculine mystique," 158-59; and child-rearing, 159-60; economic growth, 161-62; as viewed in public opinion polls, 162-63;

Pinckney, Eliza Lucas, 18
"Pin money," 31-32
Poll tax, 84
Potter, David, 148
Prescriptive norms, 10-11, 15-17, 20-21, 34-36, 94-95
"Progressive Era," 29, 124
Prohibition, 28, 82
Public opinion polls: on sex, 122; on women's liberation, 139; attitudes toward careers, 140; on equality and success, 146-48, 162-63

Race: as a central determinant in the social structure, vii-ix, 44, 45; as a basis of social control, 45ff; as analogous to sex, 58-59, 67-78, 81, 99-111; as a dividing line in support of women's liberation, 136-37
Race riots, 87
Randolph, A. Philip, 85
Rape, 66
Reform activities, 8, 24; relation to religious impulses, 24; role of women's club activities, 28
Religion, 24
Robinson, Ruby Doris Smith, 110-11
Roles, 56-57, 64-65
Roosevelt Administration, 84, 104
Roper poll, 83, 146
Rossi, Alice, 26, 51, 159

Sambo, 55-56, 138
Scott, Anne Firor, 19, 108
SDS, 97
Seneca Falls, N.Y., 25, 29, 118, 129
Seniority rights, 152
Separatism, 104-5, 109-11, 175
Settlement house, 39
Sex: as an issue analogous to race, vii, 46, 58-59, 67-78, 81, 99-111; as sexuality, 33, 45-46; interracial sex, 45-46, 110; sexual freedom, 118-19, 121-22
Sex roles: as determinant of the social structure, 3; in the 1930's, 15; impact of industrialism on, 21-24, 34-35; influence of education, 27; segregation in the work force, 31; impact of World War

II on, 92-93; persistence of traditional roles, 133-34; process of change, 145-47; and equality, 147
Sexual Suicide, 133
Sherrod, Charles, 109
"Sisterhood," 9, 56-57, 97-98, 117-18
Sit-ins, 89, 102
Skidmore College, 33
Slavery, 24, 47, 51, 55-56, 75
Small Changes, 67-72
Smelser, Neil, 99
Smith College, 27
Smith-Rosenberg, Carroll, 83
SNCC, 90, 97, 109-11
Social change, 26-27, 36-37, 77-78, 81, 122-23, 145-47, 171; alternative views of, 82; as basis for comparing sex and race, 84, 99-113; effect of World War II on blacks, 84-86, 99-100; migration as an influence, 86; effect of World War II on women, 92-95, 99-100; theme of cultural contradictions, 100-101; importance of a catalyst, 101-2; role of innovative tactics, 102-3; theme of self-definition, 104-7; relation to feminism, 117-42, especially 141-42
Social control, 42, 46, 58-78, 85, 99-100; blacks as victims of physical control, 60; as victims of economic control, 61; as victims of psychological control, 61-62; as victims of internal control, 62-63; women as victims of physical control, 66; economic control, 66-68; psychological control, 68-69; internal controls, 70-72; analogy of sex and race, 66-78
Social mobility, 149-50
Social movements, 7-8, 10, 24-26, 40, 81, 117-42
Social protest, 8; requirement of supportive community, 72-74, 81, 98
Social reform, 8, 24, 37, 82; relation to religious impulse, 24; women's clubs involvement, 28; and the Progressive era, 37, 39
Social Research, Inc., 126
"Social space," 103
Social structure: tendency to perpetuate itself, 10, 41; effectiveness in controlling blacks, 60-65; controlling women, 66-74

Socialist-feminist conference, 135-37
Socialization: as a basis for female culture, 4-5; as a means of controlling blacks and women, 58-78, especially 73-74, 104; effect of female employment on, 96; of males, 158
Southern Farmers Alliance, 131
Southern women, 16
Southerners, 62
Spectator, 16, 19
Spelman College, 109
Spruill, Julia Cherry, 19-20
Stanton, Elizabeth Cady, 44, 47, 117
Steinberg, David, 144-45
Steinem, Gloria, 138
Stevenson, Adlai, 16
Stimpson, Catharine, 47-48, 58, 108, 111
Suffrage, 29, 37-38, 40-41, 82, 117-18
Sula, 53
Supreme Court, 88, 130
Sweden, 153

Temperance, 8
Textile mills, 22-23
Theory of Collective Behavior, 99
Thompson, E.P., 3, 7
Title VII, 1964 Civil Rights Act, 96
"Total Woman" movement, 10, 134
Truman, Harry, 87-89; Committee on Civil Rights, 87; visit to Harlem, 87; election of 1948, 88; actions regarding blacks, 88
Truth, Sojourner, 124

Unequal pay, 31
Union College, 33
U.S. v. Darby, 130

Van Vechten, Carl, 50
Vassar College, 27
Voting Rights Act, 130

Wages, 31
War, 10; World War II, 84-86, 92-95, 99-100, 172
Washington, Booker T., 68
Washington, Margaret, 109

Washington, Mary Helen, 53
Wellesley College, 28
Wells, Ida Barnett, 109
Welter, Barbara, 16
Wiebe, Robert, 28
Wirth, Louis, 4, 6
Woman's "place," 7-11, 15-16, 18, 20-21, 24, 26, 29, 31, 34-37, 56, 68, 101, 104, 120, 172, 174-76; impact of industrialism, 21-24; impact of suffrage upon, 29-30; compared to blacks, 46-58, 66-72; as reinforced by economic controls, 68; impact of World War II, 94-96; persistence of traditional attitudes, 95, 147
"Woman's" work, 7-9, 29-30, 48, 50, 67, 95
Women: definition as a group, 3-4, 171, 174-75; as a minority, 4, 173-75; female culture, 4-5, 137-38, 174; women's institutions, 5, 77, 174; and ghettoes, 5-6, 51-52; colleges, 6, 26-29, 30, 37, 40-41, 68; self-perception, 6-9, 93-94, 171; and consciousness, 6-11, 40-42, 56-57, 77-78, 83, 95-97, 101-6, 109-11, 139-41; women's employment, 7, 17, 18-20; aggregate behavior, 7-9; and collective behavior, 7-11, 36-38, 40-41, 77-78, 82, 96-97, 101-6, 109-11, 139, 172; protest, 8, 24-26, 36-37, 39-40, 57, 73-75, 93-98, 101-6, 118-20, 139; education, 9, 26-29, 37; career/marriage conflict, 15, 30, 33, 155-56; in the South, 16, 68; views of marriage, 16, 110, 145, 163; the economy, 17-18, 21-24, 30-31, 34, 47-48, 66-68, 92-95, 118-19, 145; their roles in colonial America, 17-20; in careers, 18-19, 27-28, 30-33, 47, 69, 140, 145; in politics, 19, 29-30, 47, 118; immigrant women, 22-24, 28; black women, 22-24, 30-31, 35-36, 52-55, 108-12, 125; their roles in Victorian America, 26-27, 34, 118; women's clubs, 28-29; discrimination against, 28-33, 47-50, 66-72, 92-95, 97-98, 120, 147; and suffrage, 29, 36-37; as consumers, 33; and equality, 39, 57, 92-93, 96-97, 139, 156-63; absence of legal rights, 47; compared to

blacks, 47-58, 173-74; stereotypes of, 48-49; absence of common geographical base, 51, 55, 57-58, 96; differences from blacks, 51-58; as victims of social control, 66-72; and the church, 71-72; and exile, 74-75; World War II, 92-95, 172; gap between attitudes and behavior, 94; in the civil rights movement, 96-97, 101-2, 109-11; sexuality, 119-21; differential life stages, 155-56

Women Studies, 105

Women's Bureau, 32, 93

Women's Christian Temperance Union, 28

Women's clubs, 28

Women's College, Duke University, 68

Women's colleges, 27-30

Women's Equity Action League, 97, 123

Women's history, 9

Women's liberation, 8, 81, 97-106, 111-13, 118-19; social origins of, 119-23; impact of employment and demographic patterns, 120-21; as a "guerilla" movement, 123; structure of the movement, 123-26; diversity and decentralization, 123-26; political sympathies of, 125; relation to working class and black women, 125; local basis of, 127; charges of structurelessness, 127-28; variety of objectives, 129-31; activities in one community, 131; obstacles to the movement, 131-34; threat to traditional views, 132-33; male response, 134-35; internal dissension, 135-37; poll results, 139; impact on career plans, 140; on consciousness, 142, 146; and equality, 146-51, 167-68

Women's rights movement, 8, 24-29, 36-37, 41, 81, 118-19, 121, 125

Women's "sphere," 26

Women's Trade Union League, 5, 125-26

World War II: impact on blacks, 84-86, 99-100; impact on women, 92-95, 99-100, 172

Wright, Richard, 59-70, 72-75, 105

Yankelovich, Daniel, 122, 139, 161

Yellow Springs, Ohio, 135

Young people's attitudes: toward sex, 122; toward children, 161; toward success, 162-63

YWCA, 5, 108

Zero Population Growth, 121